CONVERSATIONS WITH MY MOM

Sheila Dean

ISBN 978-1-63885-781-5 (Paperback)
ISBN 978-1-63885-782-2 (Digital)

Covenant Books
11661 Hwy 707
Murrells Inlet, SC 29576
www.covenantbooks.com

INTRODUCTION

As I begin to write this book, there are some things, I need to make very clear. It is not my intention to misrepresent myself as someone highly educated in the social norms of society. I don't have advanced degrees in sociology or psychology. Every statement I make is based on life experience, common sense, mother's wit, and a whole lot of conversations with my mother and my elders. The very idea to write this book is God inspired, and the tool He has given me in response to my question, "Lord, how can I serve your people in a tangible way?" I pray this book helps keep you from some of the pains of life and adds wisdom and understanding to help you live in your purpose and in peace.

Side note: Take some time to talk to the elders in your life. There is a great deal of untapped knowledge there waiting to be harvested.

Let me take a minute to explain what motivated me to even attempt to write this book. I have a daughter, and we often talk about the things going on with her generation and those younger adults she encounters. Let me just say here that, somewhere, somebody has dropped the ball in the education of young women and some older women as well. We need to know how to live a peaceful, productive, and fulfilled life. We need to know we are beautifully and wonderfully made and that our beauty is not dependent on what we look like, what neighborhood we live in, or other people's opinions of us. You are a priceless being created by God with a purpose in this world.

Oh yeah, I know what some of you are thinking. Who died and made you queen? Here's the answer—nobody died, and I appointed myself the title of queen. I hope that by the time you finish reading this book, you will know your own royal status, your value, and what a wonderful gift you are or can be to the life of others as well as yourself. I pray you will read this book with an open mind toward becoming your best self.

I like when instruction is simple. When instruction is simple, it doesn't intimidate; it is easy to digest or take in. This makes it easier to apply and execute.

Let me again make it clear—this is a self-help book based on my life experiences. Those things that you feel have value, use them. If you don't agree, find the solution that works for you. I do not have all the answers, but I hope this book will inspire you to examine some of the choices you have made in the past and give you more insight, so your future choices will be made with greater wisdom and understanding of the dangers of lack of forethought. All decisions have consequences both good and bad. One of the perks of being an adult is you get to make your own decisions. One of the downfalls of being an adult is because you make your own decisions, you don't have anyone to blame for the outcome but yourself.

Here is my thought process: if I see you burn yourself on a hot stove, yell out in pain, and now have a burn to show evidence of your bad choice. I choose to learn from your experience. I don't need to go and touch the stove to know (1) hot burns, (2) pain has a reflex action and a voice, and (3) not thinking before you act leaves scars that can last a lifetime.

I pray this book will bless you as intended, prevent you from having to suffer the pains of bad decisions, and help you to have an honest conversation with yourself about your choices and the impact they have had and continue to have on your life.

We must develop a habit of thinking before doing. We must develop a habit of weighing the pros and cons before moving forward. We must realize that living just for the moment can impact you for a lifetime.

If, when reading this book, you avoid looking at yourself and instead use it to point out the flaws of your friends and family, you will have missed an opportunity to be a better version of yourself.

One of the most difficult things to do as an adult is to be honest with yourself. It is difficult but so necessary in order to grow in wisdom, know your worth, live in peace, and walk in your purpose.

No matter where you go in life, you cannot escape yourself, so you may as well learn how to love yourself and that begins with walking in your truth. No sugarcoating, excuse making, justifying, no rationalizing, and pretending what is ain't.

How to use this book

If you are reading this book, perhaps you have admitted to yourself that all your decisions have not been good ones. Perhaps you have a desire to do better and don't know where to start. My prayer is this book will be a stepping-stone for you to have a better, more peaceful, and happy life. But we must start with living in our own truth.

How do you use this book effectively? There are five easy but also hard steps:

1. Pray first and ask for understanding and insight that will help you.
2. Actually read just one chapter or day at a time. Make notes to yourself in the space provided. Get more paper if you need to, and put a date on your reflections.
3. Stay focused on you; don't read and say that what she (whomever she is) did, and only look at you and your choices.
4. Accept that you didn't do everything right; now forgive yourself. You are human, and we are all flawed.
5. After you recognize and are able to admit the part you played in the disruption and disappointments of your life, *do better.*

DAY 1

Be Open to Learning
I Cannot Begin to Teach You What
You Think You Already Know

One sure way to have a difficult life is to presume that you are so smart that you cannot learn from ordinary people and ordinary day-to-day situations. The other way is to refuse to be honest with yourself about your choices and the effect they have on your life. Learning is available in every situation. We must take the time to observe and be open to receive new information regardless of the source. Lessons can be learned from a newborn baby, a drunk on the street, or a college-educated professional. There are only two things in life that prevent increasing your level of knowledge and those are a refusal to admit you don't know everything and being closed-minded about who can teach you something.

Knowledge has one purpose and that is to improve your quality of life. Knowledge teaches us how to fix what is broken. Knowledge helps us problem solve. Knowledge tells you what's appropriate for the situation. Knowledge of self gives you a set of standards for your life that you can live comfortably with throughout your life. Knowledge of God and His word increases your faith walk and your wisdom. Ignorance of God's word and God's promises leaves you unprepared, confused, and even defeated or depressed.

You may be wondering about the examples I gave about the newborn and the drunk's ability to teach you. A newborn has no language, but through their cries, will make you aware when they are hungry or wet or want attention. This is a valuable lesson—to make yourself heard when you have a need. A newborn will not allow their needs to be ignored and will persist to do what is necessary to get their needs met. They have no words yet use what they do have, which is their cry, to get what is necessary for their survival and ability to thrive. So what has this newborn taught us?

1. Don't allow yourself or your needs to be ignored.
2. Make yourself heard.
3. Be persistent.
4. Be vocal about what you need in order to thrive.

The drunk on the street can teach you the consequences of not dealing with problems in a way that will promote a positive outcome. They can teach you that when you don't resolve issues, it can alter your life. They show us how unresolved issues take you to a state of being you never in your wildest dreams thought would happen to you. You can learn from observation of this person what defeat and hopelessness can look like. It is a reminder that there, but for the grace of God, go I. The song writer says, "It could have been me, outdoors with no food and no clothes…"

This book is intended to encourage you to pause and reflect on your life, your choices, and to hopefully inspire you to examine the methods you are using to get to your goals.

The college graduate also has knowledge beyond what was learned in the classroom that they have experienced. The fact that they have graduated means

1. they met the standards required of them;
2. they have a successful level of self-discipline, independent of being forced by others or their parents;
3. they set a goal for themselves and worked to achieve that goal;

4. they made a choice about what they wanted to be or do with their life and worked to put things in place so they would be successful; and

5. they did not let the distractions all around them pull them off course.

This list could go on even further, but I trust you get the idea.

No one knows everything. In order to grow, we must admit there are things we are still learning. There is no shame in mistakes while we are learning. The problem is when we make mistakes and we don't learn from them.

Open yourself up to learning, so each day you become smarter and wiser.

To become smarter, you must gather information, but to be wise, you must apply the information you have gathered. Learn to listen. Teach yourself to listen. Digest what you hear. Apply what you've learned where appropriate.

It is extremely unproductive to think that only people that are in your same age group are the only ones that can teach or understand you. A seventy-year-old person has knowledge about things that can be very beneficial to a fifteen-year-old and vice versa. Learning has two participants: the teacher and the student. These roles will fluctuate according to the situation. No matter what role you find yourself in, remember that when you are the teacher, avoid acting superior and judgmental. This attitude is demeaning and shuts down a person's ability to learn because their focus becomes defensive and often combative.

If you are the student, be open to expanding your knowledge without feeling degraded, defensive, or less than. If you assume a posture of defensiveness and resentment, you also will shut down and put up barriers against doing better in the future when challenges come your way. You can't do better if you won't allow yourself to know better.

No one can be taught what they think they already know. They have predetermined your teachings are a waste of their time because they *think* they already know it all no matter what *it* is.

Reflections

Am I open to receive new information that may be beneficial to me?

In a conversation, do I truly hear and receive what the other person is saying, or is my primary focus only to get my point across?

Is the reason I'm stuck in the same place or level of maturity and wisdom the fact that I think I already know everything I need to know about the situation?

DAY 2

When Choosing a Mate, Your Requirements Can Help or Harm You

Your life goals regarding the type of relationship you want will greatly determine what kind of choices you make. If you are looking to be taken care of by a *sugar daddy*, your focus for yourself will be looking good and presenting yourself as a sexual partner with few restrictions. You will make sure when he sees you that every lash is curled, the bra pushes you up, and in general, you are candy for the eyes. This is vitally important because you are advertising yourself to prospective clients. You have made a conscious choice to be a woman that will *lay for pay*. All prostitutes don't work corners. Do not be deceived if a man is paying your rent or car note who is not your husband; it is a financial transaction with an expectation of a return on his investment. That return is sex. A sexual relationship with a man you have no desire to marry for financial gain is prostitution. The fact that it's the same man each time instead of different men does not alter that fact.

If you've decided to be an independent woman making your own money and paying your own way, you will place more value on your education and acquiring job skills. This doesn't mean you don't want a companion, but it does mean you prefer to be responsible for your own financial security. The fact that you have put things in place for your own financial independence works to your benefit long-term. You don't have to attach yourself to someone that you've settled for because you needed help paying your bills. You are in a position to take your time and explore a relationship with someone you are compatible with and possibly interested in pursuing a relationship with long-term. If the relationship does not work, you don't have to feel trapped because you need the financial help.

If marriage is your primary goal, your efforts will be toward finding and locking down a partner. This often gets tricky, and women often find themselves compromising their standards when things don't move along as fast as they would like. We'll settle for shacking up or being a girlfriend way more years than makes us happy. Sometimes women resort to games or tricks. Oops, I'm pregnant (often more than once). We also have the games—checking his phone, tracking his phone, checking his email, calling the other woman, breaking car windows, keying his car because you're mad your games didn't work in getting him down the aisle. If you have to scheme or trick him to get him down the aisle, you will be the one in a trick bag in the marriage. When he does not choose you as his wife, he also does not emotionally commit to you as his wife. This is the very definition of *it's just a piece of paper*.

One of the most difficult things for a woman to do is self-examine. Many of the standards we have for ourselves have been placed on us by society. What other folks will think or say about the choices we make often lead us down a road that hasn't been paved, making it rough and leading to nowhere.

One of the most self-destructive types of women is the ones who won't take no for an answer. The man has made it clear he does not want them but that becomes a challenge instead of a deterrent. I have seen women do things to get and keep a man that puts them in very uncomfortable and even dangerous positions. I've got to have a man, any man because I can't have folks thinking I can't get a man. I'll be the best sex he ever had; that will keep him. Or I'll let him live with me for free; I'll totally support him like he's my child. I'll have his baby. I'll participate in threesomes. I'll buy him shoes and clothes and drugs, whatever it takes. I'll let him abuse me; I'll wait for him to get out of jail. I'll overlook his abuse of myself and my children. Just don't leave me.

Women that fall into these groups are usually in denial about the major part they are playing in their own disastrous life. They accuse the man of lying to them when in actuality, they have lied to themselves. Do you want to marry a man you had to trick, manipulate, scheme, or entrap as your husband? If he did not choose the relationship and feels tricked or trapped, the chances are very high he will not feel obligated to be faithful or committed. He will tell himself his unfaithfulness and hurtful actions are not his fault because after all, he didn't want this marriage/relationship in the first place—you did. Well, you got what you wanted, so deal with it.

When he started seeing you, he was living with or married to someone else, but you're surprised he cheated on you.

He has a history of hitting and living off women, but when he hit you and steals from you, then you want to act surprised.

You got pregnant, and he won't help physically or financially with the baby, but he has five other kids that he does nothing for and doesn't have any contact with; yet you want to act surprised because he doesn't help with your child.

No one has an expectation of seeing a dog fly south for the winter because that's what birds do. Dogs behave as dogs; how ridiculous it is to expect bird behavior from a dog. Identify what you are working with honestly and then govern yourself accordingly based on what you want for your life.

When choosing a life partner, there are some women that have a list. A list is only as good as the items it contains. If in choosing a partner your list is superficial, that's what you'll end up with—a superficial, unreliable, lazy, no-work ethic, having a mooch. You may be asking what is a superficial list. That list may contain elements like cute, tall, fancy car, fancy clothes, fancy job, will buy me stuff, or take me places. Maybe you want him to be impressive to your friends or have a large penis and so on and so forth. If this is what your list contains, you are so not ready for a serious relationship because you are totally clueless about what sustains a relationship.

Now having said that, if all you want is a good time with one man after another after another, then your list is perfection.

I, in no way, am the deciding factor in how you want to live your life, but if you are looking to have a long-term, committed relationship with one person, the list should look very different. That list may contain things like kind, hard worker, dependable, responsible, honest, loving, supportive, godly, great sense of humor, slow to anger, respectful, and fun to be with. Your partner is an enhancement to your life; it is not their job to complete you. You need to be a complete individual when you meet them. You should have your own dreams, goals, standards, and opinions. You should already know what is and is not acceptable to you. You should know what your deal breakers in a relationship are. What makes you happy and what are you likely to do when someone crosses the line with you? These revelations come with time and *self-reflection* and *prayer*.

As I write this, let me pause here to make something very clear. I am not telling you how to live your life, but I am trying desperately to give you food for thought that will hopefully spare you a great deal of grief and heartbreak. There will be very few absolutes that I will try to get you to follow, but I will advise you strongly about this one thing. *Never put yourself in a position where if a man puts you out, is abusive to you and/or your children, that you feel/believe that you can't/won't make it without him.*

Reflections

How much does your desire to take the easy road affect how you choose a partner

How much does what your friends think affect the choice of man you select for yourself?

Have you unconsciously decided that any man is better than no man?

Do you have the qualities you are asking for that man to have?

DAY 3

Who Are You?

Your standards for your life cover many areas. One of these areas is your individuality. We have all been designed to be different from everybody else. God has created no two human beings exactly the same. If you are an exact duplicate of someone, one of you is unnecessary. Have you allowed conforming to the world's standards determine your choices, your clothing, who your friends are, and the very level of your self-confidence? Have you allowed yourself to be shut down by the comments of others and a need for their approval? Have you allowed discouraging words to prevent you from pursuing your dreams?

In order to have your own set of standards, you must acquire the strength to walk by your own set of rules. You must be prepared to stand in your own truth even when your friends, family, and enemies don't agree with your chosen path. As an adult, maturity and self-confidence give you the ability to retain your joy and peace when others don't agree with your choices. When you cannot stand in your own truth, you set yourself up to become a people pleaser at the cost of your own peace. You will also become a follower, letting others lead you down the path they have chosen for you. This leads you to find yourself in situations you may not be able to get out of or that will leave lasting scars you could have avoided if you had just stood for what was right for you instead of others. Every decision you make won't necessarily be the right decision, but we learn through experience, and with a healthy degree of forethought, we will usually make good choices.

Everyone needs to set standards for themselves. If you have no goals, aspirations, and plans for your life, they will be assigned to you by those in your life. Everyone you encounter does not wish you well; many people you encounter will be in competition with you. (Every competition has a winner and a loser. Guess which one they want to be? If they win, you have to lose.)

Do you know anyone that tried drugs because their friends talked them into it? Were you encouraged to go along so you could get along and be accepted by the group? How many people have been to prison for not having the strength of character to walk away from the crowd because they would be teased or put down?

Were you talked into having sex before you were ready? Did you again go along to get along? He said, "If you love me, you will do it." You can't get pregnant the first time. What are you saving it for? Nobody will know (until he tells his friends to brag at your expense).

Let's shoplift out this store. Let's cuss out that old lady; what is she going to do? Let's sneak out of the house or cut school. For the rest of your life, there will be someone in your life trying to tell you to do the wrong thing, and if you have no standards *for yourself,* they will mold you like clay to whatever suits their needs with no thought of how your life will be changed or impacted. They also will be the same people that when you are knee-deep in trouble will walk away and leave you to fend for yourself.

One of the most important things you will do in life is to find your own identity. This may require you to spend some time alone. Alone is not a bad thing and is actually necessary for growth. We need time to review the things we've done. We need time to assess was it a good choice, and if not, what could I have done differently? Additionally, since I made a choice that did not work out for me, what can I learn so I don't repeat this same mistake?

No matter what others think of you, the consequences of your choices will be either paid for by you or the benefits will be reaped by you. We want to win more than we lose.

Set standards for yourself and stick to them! There are major consequences if you don't and let others do it instead of you.

Reflections

Are you happy with who you are? If not, what are you doing to change it?

Do you let other people make decisions for your life even if you don't agree with them?

In an effort to get along or be accepted, do you compromise your values or principles?

Are you prepared to walk away rather than not walk in the truth of who you are and what you feel comfortable participating in?

DAY 4

Relationship Standards: What Are You Inviting into Your Life?

Remember I told you standards cover many areas of your life. Well, one of the areas is your relationships with others, particularly a romantic relationship.

There are basically three kinds of relationships: family, friends, and love life.

Family relationship

These relationships should be loving, caring, and supportive, but that is not always the case. These relationships are where we learn to love, learn what love looks like, and we learn how to interact with others. Sadly, many people come from dysfunctional or totally unsupportive homes. This creates a whole set of problems. When a home is not a secure place where you feel safe, protected, and loved unconditionally, it will affect your relationships. In many relationships, the parents or caregivers transfer their baggage to their children, and now the children carry the baggage into their relationships. This baggage comes in many different ways. You may have an inability to trust others, leading you to be insecure and suspicious of others. You may be overly aggressive if you witnessed violence or constant bickering in your home growing up.

One of the problems with this baggage is you may not even realize you are carrying it. You may be carrying so much anger, resentment, and attitude from past hurts or disappointments from your family. You have been mentally altered and often are totally unaware this has even happened because it's all you know.

Damaged people will require some extra work to not repeat these patterns in their future relationships. If you are in a relationship with someone who is a victim of a damaging family life and you want to pursue that relationship long-term, the road will not be easy, and the challenges will be difficult. We must make every effort to maintain positive relationships within our family. You will judge the rest of the world by the things you experienced at home when growing up.

However, know this—too much time spent with toxic people will pollute you and your future. *Learn to love from a distance when necessary.* This does not mean cut your family off, don't answer their calls, or be there for them, but it does mean protect your peace. You will have to learn to know the difference between being helpful and being used. Don't argue! An argument is one person trying to force another person to think what they think. We are individuals with our own thoughts. When possible, compromise, but if no compromise can be reached, move on in peace, and be your best self.

Friends

Don't be so quick to label someone as your friend who has not proven themselves. Hanging out with someone, working together, going to school together, or knowing the same people does not make a person your friend. Can they pass the friend test? Have they passed the friend test?

Before you call them your friend, here are a few questions you may want to think about before you award the title of *friend*:

1. When they talk about you, is the conversation the same when you are out of the room as it is when you are in the room?

2. Are they telling you other people's secrets that were confided in them as a friend? If they are telling their secrets, they're telling yours too. Side note: My grandmother used to have a saying that said, "If it's a secret about you and you can't keep it on yourself, why would you expect anybody else to keep it?" Food for thought.

3. Has your friend shared times they plotted or schemed to get revenge on someone and enjoyed telling you how clever they were? This is a vindictive person, and they should not be trusted. They are letting you know if you cross me, I will deliberately put a plan in motion to cause harm to you because I am a vengeful person. It's a warning you need to keep in mind.

4. Are they there for you when you need them without the mindset or attitude that now you owe them a debt in return? This is not support; this is a secret contract of obligation that you may not even know you're entering. Let me make it plain. Old folks call it tit for tat. You will hear younger people say, "You owe me." Their help came with a price tag. If you are calling someone your friend yet every time they do something for you they have an expectation of a favor in return, tread carefully. This is a person with a what's-in-it-for-me? mindset.

5. Does your friend celebrate when good things happen to you, or do they become jealous? Jealousy will manifest itself in several ways. They may try to sabotage your plans, begin to lie or gossip about how you got what you got, or they may try to bring you down or minimize your accomplishment. *Do not* underestimate the evil that lurks in a jealous heart. A jealous person will plot against you, lie on you, try to destroy you, and do these things while smiling in your face and pretending they are not making plans to destroy you.

6. Are you unevenly yoked? *Unevenly yoked* is a biblical term basically which means not on the same page. Is what's important to you also important to your friend? Do your

values match? Are your standards compatible with each other? Remember, I said some people you have to love from a distance. An unevenly yoked relationship will always be a tug-of-war. Let me say that again—an unevenly yoked relationship will always be a tug-of-war. You will either be trying to pull them to your way of thinking or they will try to pull you to theirs. People taking the low road spend a great deal of their time trying to pull people off the high road. The saying misery loves company is real. A person involved in criminal activity will try to enlist you to partic-ipate also. A person involved in an extramarital affair will give you all the reasons it's justified. A person who thinks church is a scam to get your money and all preachers are no good church pimps will take every opportunity to talk you out of going to church. Trust me on that. Name one person you know that tried drugs and didn't try to influence or pressure others to try them as well.

Make your own list of questions that are important to you as a check and balance for how you would define who is a true friend. Very few people in your life will ever truly earn the title of *true friend*. Remember, to keep a friend you also have to be a friend. A selfish friendship will only last for a little while, and you will have lost something very precious if you continually take from a relationship that you are not giving anything to.

Reflections

Will you allow someone to walk all over you in order to keep them as a friend? Have you done this if you were honest with yourself?

Have you compromised yourself to be accepted by certain people or groups? You may have done this as a child, but are you still doing it as an adult?

Do you allow others to destroy your peace of mind?

How do you handle betrayal and repeat offenders that hurt you?

DAY 5

Secret vs. Personal: Keep Your Business off Social Media

How much of your business are you willing to share and why? Many times, when people become comfortable, they begin to share things about their life with the wrong people. They also share things that don't need to be shared. When you open the door and let folks into the most intimate parts of your life, you also open the door to someone sticking their nose in your business. No one can spread or comment on your business if you stop telling it to them.

When you walk down the aisle and get married, it is pretty much understood the couple will engage in sexual relations. It's not a secret, but it is personal. You don't need to share what you and your spouse do in bed, the size of his penis, the frequency or location of your sexual activity. *That is nobody's business. Keep your relations and relationship private.* You tell your friends how good your partner is in bed; well, you are going to stimulate their curiosity, and you may look up and suddenly, you've got competition for their affection. They may never have thought of your man in a sexual way but you keep planting the seed of interest and the seed of jealousy. Girl, let me tell you what you are missing. Be careful of the seeds you plant; somebody will water them to see how they grow.

You're having problems in your relationship, and so, in your anger, you bad-mouth your partner and call them everything but a child of God. You make all kinds of empty threats about what you are going to do and what you're not going to put up with under any circumstances. It's two years later, and you're still in the relationship. It's ten years later, and you're still right there in the same relationship. They're doing the same things they were doing when you sold all the empty threats. Well guess what; now that friend is talking all about what a fool you are. Understand their conversation will be about how much smarter they are than you because they wouldn't put up with it. They will talk about how they would have done this or that, but you're just too weak and stupid. Well guess what; your big mouth gave them the gossip gun, loaded it, and then painted a target on your back. Now you're mad because they took their shot. They have shared your personal business with several people with whatever embellishments would make it juicier. You told all your personal business, which should have been kept personal, until and even after you decided what you were going to do about your relationship. Girl, shut up, be quiet, and tell Jesus. He never gossips and will give you direction if you'll just ask Him.

Personal

The first part of the word *personal* is person, singular. This means one. The people you share your personal life with should not be able to fill a lecture hall or even a car. You cannot get angry when others won't do for you what you didn't do for yourself and that's keep your personal business personal.

Secrets

Secret, by its very definition, means to not reveal the unknown. Often secrets come with a level of danger or potential harm. We should not keep secrets when someone is in danger. When do we break the code of silence? There is a difference between personal and secret. *Personal* means to keep private while *secret* means to hide or conceal information.

Some examples of secrets are domestic abuse, child molestation, drug abuse, and more. If the secret you are keeping allows someone to be abused, molested, and generally endangered, you become a silent partner and support the situation by keeping these behaviors secret. You could have stopped that child from being abused, but you hid the secret and allowed the abuse to continue. Your secrecy has made you an accomplice in the crime. Before revealing a secret, verify it is true and examine whether the reveal will be beneficial or harmful. Words have tremendous power and once spoken cannot be unspoken.

Social media is *forever*. It does not matter if you delete your post. Once you post your personal business on social media, it is available to everyone. This includes your parents, their friends, your church, your employer, your old and new boyfriend, and every hacker on the planet. The fact that your page is private does not keep it from being hacked and the information used against you. We have to get in the habit of thinking long-term. This includes that video you made for him, those pictures you took for him. What will he do with them when he gets mad at you, or you break up? Will he show all his friends, send them to your parents, maybe even post them on a porn site? Don't give folks weapons to use against you.

Keep your business off Facebook, Instagram, TikTok, and all other social media. Every picture you send to his or her phone can be uploaded or forwarded to anybody anywhere. I want you to consider how fast a post can go viral and be viewed by over ten million people. Have you sent pictures or made videos that you would be okay with being viewed by ten million or even ten thousand people? When a post is taken down, there is no guarantee it has not been saved on someone's device, in the cloud, or any other medium. Keep your business off of social media. When you post you are out of town now, I know your house is empty—a burglar's dream. You tell me you're at the restaurant while you are still there. If I am looking for you for a vengeful reason, you've told me where to find you. Why are you telling me on social media you came into some money? Do you want to get set up and robbed? The information you share without thinking can have dangerous consequences. Everybody doesn't need to know everything about you.

Reflections

If it's a secret and you can't keep it on yourself, why do you have an expectation that someone else will keep it if you couldn't and it's about you?

What kind of approval are you seeking that you need to let everyone know the who, what, when, and where of your life?

Why are you angry when others have so much gossip to say about you when you are the one giving them all the information?

Are you sharing personal information for the approval of others or because you're in competition with them, and it's your way of keeping score?

DAY 6

Pick a Shoe, the Mary Jane Woman

What does it mean when I say pick a shoe? I'm glad you asked. When we are little girls and we would get all dressed up for special occasions, our moms would put us on a shiny pair of patent leather Mary Jane shoes that buckled on the side. We knew we were dressed up because we only wore these shoes for special stuff like church or school pictures. As we got older and wanted to be more grown-up, we would put on Momma's heels and pretend we were all grown-up. The shoes were too big for us, and we often would trip and fall. We would fall because we were walking in a grown woman's shoes, but we only had kid's shoe skills. We were pretending to be something we were not. We had Mary Jane knowledge, Mary Jane experience, and Mary Jane references. We were pretending. The problem with this is once you put on the stilettoes like a grown woman, the expectation is that you will conduct yourself as a woman.

You will solve problems like a grown woman, handle uncomfortable situations like a woman, resolve disagreements like a woman, take care of yourself like a woman, and depend on yourself rather than having the expectation or delusion that somebody owes you something.

When we are children, our parents provide shelter, clothing, and food. They protect us from bullies and dig us out of the holes we sometimes get in through our choices. They make us do our homework and our chores. They make you go to bed so you won't be tired at school, and they celebrate our accomplishments. But you're no longer in Mary Janes. Older people often used the phrase, "Put on your big girl panties." This was a colorful way of saying grow up and handle your business.

There are too many women that want to straddle the fence between adulthood and being a child. When you don't want to be told what to do, you're grown. However, when you buy that Coach purse instead of paying your electric bill, now you want to be treated like a little girl and have someone else handle your responsibilities so you're not sitting in the dark. You want to be treated like you're still a little girl with your shiny patent leather Mary Janes.

When you were a little girl, you used one set of tactics to get your way, and now as an adult, you use a different method although some of them will overlap. As a little girl, maybe you would have a temper tantrum, maybe you used guilt. ("Susie's mom let her go or let her have a new doll.") Then there's the number one tactic on the how-can-I-manipulate-you? hit list. The tears, the big cry because you are just so upset. You see, maybe if I make you feel sorry for me, you'll give me what I want and then I'll be all better, at least until next time.

Please understand other tactics for manipulation come into play when you put on the big girl shoes. Women will manipulate things in several ways when they want to get taken care of like a child but respected as a woman. YOU CAN'T HAVE IT BOTH WAYS! The Mary Jane women will challenge your manhood and accuse you of not being a man if you can't give her what she wants. She may try to get it from another man, she will lie, scheme, and the oldie but goodie either give or withhold sex.

A Mary Jane woman tries to keep one foot in childhood and one foot in adulthood. I repeat—you can't be a woman and a child. At some point, you have to pick a shoe and wear it.

Reflection

Do you lay traps to get your way?

Do you make bad choices and then have an expectation of someone else cleaning up your mess?

Do you make decisions that will gratify you in the moment without considering the long-term effects?

Are you in a relationship with your partner because he makes you happy or because he's another source of income? Is he your backup for your bad financial decisions?

DAY 7

Romance Versus Real Love

When we are growing up as little girls, often stories are read to us such as "Cinderella" and "Sleeping Beauty" and they always end with, "… and they lived happily ever after." They never contain disagreements, money problems, family issues, or anything that keeps us from believing love is always a picture of perfection. We are encouraged to believe that a ring and a white dress will rescue you from everything and everybody that would do you harm.

We get a little older, and now we have movies that show images of the perfect man. He is never fat, he's always good-looking, he has a great job, says all the right things, and gives you his undivided attention. He buys you flowers and gifts. He takes you to nice restaurants and never forgets any special occasions. He never ever looks at other women and thinks everything about you is all that he will ever need. This all leads to the walk down the aisle in a beautiful white dress and a fancy party that's picture perfect. If you believe these movies, your expectation is a beautiful home where women clean house in heels, their hair is always perfect, and the children are healthy and good students. All is right with the world.

I sit here with a pin in my hand as I willingly and unwillingly need to burst your bubble and give you a reality check.

Love is not a movie. Love is work, a commitment to work to stay together with forever being the goal. Love is sacrificial, love compromises. Love protects, love tries to resolve problems in a way that both parties win. Love is work. Love is the little things you know about your mate that no one else knows because they don't share the same level of intimacy. That's intimacy, not sex.

Side note: If you don't understand that intimacy and sex are two different things, you already have a problem.

When you love someone, one of the greatest ways to show that love is to pay attention to the things that may seem so small to you but those little things become a priority because they're important to your mate.

Let me break that down by giving you an example from my childhood. When I was growing up, we always, and I do mean always, had two pitchers of Kool-Aid in the refrigerator. My father worked outdoors. and sometimes the heat was extreme. And when he came home from work, all he wanted when he came in the door was something cold to drink. My mom knew everybody else gets hot too. In order to make sure there was enough for everybody without having my father come home and get disappointed, we kept two pitchers made at all times. The rule was, when one is empty, make another pitcher so there is always a cold one.

Now somebody that just missed the whole point of what I just said is saying to themselves, "Hell, if it wasn't cold, just put some ice in it."

Let me explain the difference. When Dad comes in from work and Mom has made sure he had something cold to drink, it is something she did *for him* because it made him happy. She put forth an *effort to please him* for him. He sees she has implemented rules in their home to make it more *comfortable for him*. She's saying, by her actions, "I *appreciate you* and your contributions to me and your family." She has made sure to keep a supply of sugar and Kool-Aid in the house because *it's important to him and keeps peace in the home*. Yes, he can put ice in a glass and pour the Kool-Aid and wait for it to chill enough to cool him off. You say, what's the difference? The difference is when the cold drinks are already there waiting for him, they remind him somebody loves him enough to make sure his desires for just a cold drink are being met just because it makes him happy.

When he has to put ice in a glass and wait for the drink to get cold, his desire was not met. He didn't get to feel appreciated for what he does, and his house was a little less welcoming. Love pays attention to the needs, desires, likes and dislikes of your partner. Love is in those little details that are important to your partner, so you make them important to you because you love them.

I recognize some will miss the metaphor of the Kool-Aid, but you can't help everybody. In all probability, these will be the same ones that put ketchup on his fries because that's how you eat them. You've never paid attention that when you go out for fast food, he never puts ketchup on anything. He orders his burger with no ketchup, but it's all about you. If you pay attention to the details of what makes him happy, if he is a man of quality, he will also pay attention to the things that make you happy and do his best to give them to you.

We have allowed ourselves to get so caught up in the movie version of what a relationship looks like we often miss what we have. You are fussing and cussing because he didn't give you flowers for your birthday, but when he comes over, he makes sure to tank up your car before he leaves. He didn't notice your hair, but he fixed that leak under your sink after working all day. He couldn't get off work on your birthday, so you had to wait to celebrate with him, but he sent you and a friend to dinner at his expense or maybe for mani-pedis.

Love will stay when and if you become incapacitated, gain weight, or have health problems; romance will not. Love will sacrifice and compromise rather than having to have everything your way. Romance many times is simply motivated by or used as a method to get to sex, particularly if no feelings are involved. Lust is a powerful motivator, but it is not to be confused with love. Romance, if unsuccessful, will move to the next person because they're not interested in putting in that much work or a commitment. Love has a goal of being in the relationship for a lifetime; romance is for a right-now, feels-good moment or moments.

When love motivates romantic gestures, it is an act of appreciation. When lust motivates romance, it is an act of anticipation for gratification.

Here is some food for thought: *If your man sees a problem in your life that is causing you some level of distress or discomfort and it becomes his goal to fix it in order to restore your peace, sweetheart, that is love and a strong indication he cares. He is addressing your needs first. He knows the role of a man as a provider and helpmate.*

Everyone wants to be pampered and movie-version romanced from time to time. I am not saying there is anything wrong with that. What I am saying is don't ignore the fact that the way people express love comes in many forms. Everyone expresses themselves differently; this is one of the reasons paying attention to your partner is so important.

Sometimes we are so busy looking for the big, straight-out-the-movies gestures that we miss all those small things that can carry so much heart and romance.

Have you ever spent days looking for something you get frustrated, angry, and disheartened, and then suddenly there it is? You've looked over it, all around it, and it was right under your nose. Are you spending so much time looking for the dream man that you are overlooking the man right in front of you? You know the one you've always been able to depend on, the one who always has your back, and the one who has always been a loyal friend to you. The one you can talk to about anything, and he won't judge you. Real love will never look like the movies or fairy tales. It will have ups and downs, joy, anger, and everything in between. Love is not sustained merely by romantic gestures but hard work. Love requires sacrifice. If there is no sacrifice, there is no love.

I know by now you are probably about sick of me saying love requires sacrifice, but here is the reason I've said it over and over. If you say you love someone and it never even crosses your mind to put their needs ahead of yours at least some of the time, it is not love. Let me give you an example. If you have one sandwich and your child is hungry and so are you, who gets the sandwich? If the answer is your child, you made a sacrifice because of love. If your child loses their hat and it's cold outside, and you take your hat and give it to them knowing they may lose it as well but you don't want them to get sick, that's sacrificial love. If you are not *willing* to sacrifice, love cannot be sustained even if he buys you the entire florist.

Reflections

What are five words that describe love for you?

What are five things important to sustaining a good relationship?

What are your deal breakers for ending a relationship?

Is the definition of romance the same for everyone? Does your definition match up with your partner's?

Are romance and sex the same thing?

DAY 8

Was It a Moment or a Pattern?

Are you a woman that sets yourself up for disappointment in your relationships? In our minds, we all have a list of the character traits we would like our man to have that are pleasing to us. We want him to be considerate of our feelings, romantic, strong, and so on and so forth. What happens in your mind and in your actions when there is an area where you feel he falls short of the goals you have for him? Do you take that as an opportunity to belittle him or compare him to other men? Do your actions and your mouth make the situation worse or better? I have an expression I use when describing pushing people beyond their reasonable limits. I always say everyone has an *enough button*. Children have it; animals and both women and men have as well. There are things in life we do not like done to us, and we will only tolerate for a time and then we react. The reaction you get greatly depends on how hard and how often you have tapped on our enough button.

One of the hardest things sometimes is in the midst of an argument or disagreement to either walk away or at the very least disengage and just stop talking. There is a time to challenge, and there should be an awareness in you when you need to back up and be quiet. This does not mean your opinions are not valid; it just means this is not the time to be forceful. When the atmosphere is highly volatile, not having the discernment of knowing when to back off can be dangerous and even deadly. Keep in mind there is nothing that lowers the level of a conversation like the raising of voices. If you are both screaming, no one is listening to learn; they are only listening to prepare their next response. The goal has become being right instead of being understood and resolving the problem.

It is extremely important to know how to speak up and equally important to know when to shut up. Don't let having to have the last word in an argument cause those to be your last words in life.

Sometimes, women in the midst of a very aggressive argument with a person, particularly a man, will begin hitting or pushing him. Some women feel justified in slapping a man across his face when they are angry. This is very dangerous territory. If you provoke a person to violence by attacking them, you can't suddenly play victim if/ when they hit or push you back.

When you provoke violence by losing self-control, you don't have the right to be angry when the person you provoke also loses self-control. If yours is understandable, so is theirs. Now you're hysterical, and you want to label the person as abusive. You go and tell everybody he hit you, maybe you call the police, but you never admit your part.

Here is one of the great realities of life—if you jump into the ocean, you are going to get wet. If you push a person—man, woman, or child—beyond their breaking point by not recognizing when to get your hands off their *enough button*, you have pulled that person out of their normal character into a moment when they may lose control.

When a person is out of control, their character has been altered by anger and continued frustration, leading them down a path that is not their normal behavior.

This moment is not a pattern for them, but if you tell the same story over and over, others may think it's a pattern for that person.

We all have moments in our life we are not proud of and where we wish we could get a do-over.

As a woman, it is wise to choose a man that has good patterns or habits in his life rather than a series of repeatedly uncontrolled or violent behaviors. A person's patterns for life reveal who they really are, but when provoked, we've all had our moments.

If you cannot forgive these moments and you don't want to be on the receiving end of pushing someone beyond their reasonable limits, certainly make it a practice not to provoke them.

Let me be very clear that I am not making excuses for abusive behavior or saying abuse is acceptable. Let me also be clear this applies to men and women. Keep your hands to yourself at all times. If you don't want them to hit you, start by not hitting them. Model what you want for yourself.

Reflections

Have you gone too far verbally or physically during an argument? If yes, did you learn from it?

Do you have enough self-control to walk away from an argument especially without getting in one more jab or verbal attack?

When you have a disagreement, are you interested in what the other person's side may be on the matter?

DAY 9

Are We Friends or Competitors

Friend is a word people use to identify another person in their life, but it is not always the appropriate choice. The word *friend* carries with it a level of responsibility. When you are classified as a friend, people will have certain expectations of you. Sometimes we assign this title way too early in the relationship. We use it casually when in reality not everyone you spend time with is a friend. Some of the people in your life are just passing through; some are there because an association with you provides some benefit in one area or another. Some people are friends to someone you know, and your paths just happen to cross because you have that person in common.

A true friend needs to meet certain criteria to earn that title. A true friend has the same thing to say about you whether you are in the room or in another state. A friend is loyal but at the same time will tell you if they think you are doing the wrong thing or making bad choices. A friend doesn't put you on the shelf like a pair of old shoes because they are so sure you'll always be there. They don't neglect you until they decide to throw you a bone. A friend's treatment of you is consistent regardless of who is around.

When you have a real friend, you don't have to pretend with them. If you are financially struggling, you can tell them without fear of embarrassment or criticism. A friend will keep your confidences, let you cry on their shoulder, walk with you through the difficult times, and will have you laughing so hard you have to take off running to the bathroom so you don't wet your pants.

A friend is happy with your successes because they are not in competition with you, and they want to see you do well. A friend is both comforting and encouraging when things are not going well. When you fall, a friend will help pick you up without the "I told you not to do it" or the putdowns because they accept your imperfections in the love that they have for you.

You can let a friend see you with your wig off and no makeup. You'll open the door for a friend when you haven't had time to clean the house or wash the dishes. Real friends become extended family. You can relax with them and be your authentic self without the window dressing and no pretense.

There are those among us that are under the impression we are good friends, but the evidence points in the opposite direction. You are constantly trying to one up them, you spread their business, you constantly criticize, and assume a superior posture whenever you have a success. You want them to be successful but not quite as successful as you. It's okay if they look good but not better than you.

You can have a man as long as I've got one too. If I don't have a man and you do, then I'll spend my time trying to break you up or talking bad about him or even worse, going after him for myself. I say we're friends but you can't one up me. Our friendship is contingent on you not outdoing me in any area of life. As long as I see myself as ahead of you, then we can be friends.

Beware of wolves in sheep's clothing; the bite is no less deadly because of the pretense of being something they are not.

Reflections

What qualities should a friend possess? Do you possess them?

Have you ever ignored the sign or red flags that a person may not really be your friend? How did that work out?

Have you learned what is important to you in a relationship, or do you go with the flow?

Do you know what your standards are in a relationship?

DAY 10

Just Because You're Smart Doesn't Mean You're Wise

Very often in today's society you will run across a group of people that are so very impressed with themselves and their level of education. They will proudly boast of the particular college they attended and the various degrees they have earned as a way to verify how smart they are to you. Let me be clear that there is nothing wrong with being proud of what you have achieved, but you should not be prideful. There is a difference.

Now having said that, let me make this very clear to you. An education will impart knowledge on various subject matter that is useful when applied to executing certain tasks that can lead to successful employment and financial security.

The mistake people often make is to think that being educated and being wise are the same thing. They are not.

Wisdom requires a level of problem-solving skills seldom found in books and is gained through some of life's most difficult experiences. Wisdom finds a way to get it done when you don't have a formal education. Wisdom will observe those that know how to do it, so they can draw from other folk's knowledge. Wisdom will figure out how to feed eight people with food for five and leave everybody in the table full. Wisdom teaches you when to speak up and when to shut up. Wisdom keeps you from repeating the same mistakes over and over because you learned from them. Wisdom does not accept all advice but will, at the very least, include it in the equation as information to be factored in toward the best results. Wisdom does not dismiss advice because of who it came from.

Wisdom is often underrated and a word applied to old people. There is never a great deal of celebration of wise people. There are no graduation ceremonies yet it is wise people that raise educated people to be able to achieve. In their wisdom, they figured out how to send their children to college even with the meager wages and their limited education. Wise people are survivors, innovative, and persistent. Wise people recognize what a lack of formal education cost them, so they make it a priority for their children.

No degrees are given for being wise, but the wisdom used in directing a child's behavior, selection of friends, and discipline when making bad choices lead to those degrees. Wisdom recognizes the importance of planting seeds and supporting growth toward a brighter future.

No matter how educated you are, wisdom will motivate spending time with those that have improved your life because of the wisdom they imparted in you. It directs you toward being your best self.

Reflections

Honestly, are you too impressed with yourself?

Are there people you consider beneath you intellectually? If yes, do you feel they can teach you anything?

Do you narrow the type of people you associate with based on their education, job, income, or place in the community?

Would you be in a relationship with someone less educated than you?

DAY 11

If He Wants to Be Caught, You Won't Have to Chase Him He'll Stop and Wait on You

Think back to when you were a kid and more than anything, you wanted your mom or dad to take you to McDonald's. You could just taste that cheeseburger and fries. You knew your meal came with a toy you could show your friends, and they would want one too. You would be the envy of all your friends because everybody loved McDonald's. Mom would tell you, "Baby, we're having spaghetti for dinner, and we'll get McDonald's another time."

You love your mom's spaghetti, but you wanted McDonald's. Since you're a kid, you had to eat the spaghetti. This is the same spaghetti you love, but today it's what you had to settle for. It didn't satisfy you; it didn't taste as good as it usually does because you didn't choose it. It was not what you wanted; it was what somebody else decided, and you tolerated it.

When a woman puts herself in a position where a man has made it clear he does not want you as his woman or his wife and you continue to pursue him, you will become a woman who is not desired but tolerated or settled for. You become the unwanted plate of spaghetti that satisfied the hunger but not the desire.

Will he have sex with you? Most of the time, yes, but it's because he's horny and you are available, so he settles for you if he can't get who he wants. He will feel no remorse because you pursued him even after he made it clear he wasn't interested in anything long-term with you. When you get your feelings hurt because you saw him with *her*, he'll tell you, "You knew the deal from the start. We didn't do anything you didn't want to do."

You, not him, put yourself in a position to be used as a means to an end, his sexual gratification. Why are your feelings hurt? You were doing the same thing, using sex to trap him into a relationship with you. You are angry because you are being rejected at the same time you're being used and you knew it. You're mad because he played the game better than you, and you allowed yourself to be used by someone who had already made it clear they didn't want a future with you.

When he desires you, chooses you, appreciates you, and wants to be with you, he behaves differently. You are his chosen one and not just Ms. Better Than Nothing or Ms. She'll Do in a Pinch.

If you choose to let a man know you are interested in him yet he shows no interest in you, a decision has to be made. Is better than nothing the position you want in his life? Is until someone better comes along the goal you had for the relationship?

You don't have to chase a man that wants to be caught; he'll stop and wait on you and even turn completely around and walk toward you instead of away from you. If he didn't choose you, he will still use you.

Reflections

Did he lie to you, or did you lie to yourself?

Would it be okay if a man you were not interested in continually pushed himself into your life?

Do you think it's acceptable to manipulate a person into a relationship? If you get used by that person you are manipulating, who is at fault?

If you continue to fight to keep this unwanted relationship, are you fighting for the relationship or against the rejection?

DAY 12

I Don't Play House Anymore

Everything we do in life involves making choices. The choices you make will reveal themselves whether you like or not. They will reveal themselves when you least expect it, and there will be no one to blame but yourself. I have known many women who are currently *shacking up* or living with their boyfriends. They often, in so many cases, are living with them because they want to be married and that offer has not been put on the table as an option. So this is where those choices come in. Do you settle for the shack up, press for a wedding, then move on to the next relationship or convince yourself that the marriage license is *just a piece of paper*? Let's examine the choices.

You decided to shack up, so how will the dynamics of the relationship break down? Do you share the bills fifty-fifty? Is your name the only one on all the bills and the lease? If only your name is listed and the bill hasn't been paid, who are the collection people coming after? Does he give you a flat amount each month with no adjustments regardless of the fluctuation in expenses? Are you doing his laundry like a wife? Are you having sexual relations and preparing his meals like a wife? Are you helping him raise children from another woman like a wife? Do you take care of his business and take care of him when he is ill like a wife? You are not his woman, sweetheart, you're the help. You have reduced yourself to financial support, housekeeping, and being a friend with benefits. Is that what you were dreaming of for yourself?

Do you press for a wedding? Do you want to marry someone that has no desire to commit to you? When people are forced into a corner, they usually do one of two things. They come out the corner swinging or tell you what you want to hear so you'll have hope of a change and continue to wait for the change that doesn't come. Understand that even if you convince them to marry you, they won't be faithful or committed. They will justify their actions by saying, "You're the one that wanted this marriage, not me."

Was that your dream? Do you want to have to convince someone to marry you like you're applying for a job? What does that do for your self-esteem?

Does he give you a lump sum payment each month? Here's the trick in lump sum payments. A lump sum payment says without saying it, "Look, this is what I'm giving you and don't ask for anything else. The rest of whatever else you need is on you and not my problem."

Is this always the case? Absolutely not; however, most of the time it is. You have now been reduced from a relationship to a bill or obligation. That lump sum payment you got with no regard as to the expenses was *hush money.*

Shut up and leave me alone. He gave you $400 but the rent is $900, the gas and electric bill are another $350, and you still have the phone bill, groceries, gas for the car, the sink is leaking, etc. But you already know you're not getting another dime. You see, he already paid his bill, and that bill is you. Is this the dream? This is one of the consequences of a forced marriage; you'll get just enough participation and contribution to the household to shut you up.

Is it time to move on to a new relationship? The term *new relationship* may be misleading. Many times, women will repeat the same relationship just with a different person. If you find yourself drawn to the same type of person over and over, you are not learning from your mistakes. You don't go outside in two feet of snow in flip flops; you put on socks and boots to protect yourself from harm. We must learn to protect ourselves from those people and things that will do us harm. Sometimes you need to spend some time in relationship with yourself, so you can reflect on your choices and learn from your mistakes. This will help you keep your dreams from becoming nightmares.

If the marriage license is *just* a piece of paper, why are they trying so hard to avoid having their name with your name on that simple paper?

A marriage license symbolizes a public and legal acknowledgment to the world that you have *chosen* to commit yourself to one person. You have willingly accepted this person as your partner for life in accordance with both God's law and man's law. The vows say, "For better, for worse, in sickness and in health, for richer, for poorer, till death do us part." Not every marriage will end with death, but the point is, you are going into the marriage with the intention and commitment to have forever as your goal.

If all their energy is being put into avoiding this type of commitment, they have decided to keep one foot in the relationship and one foot out. They want to keep your options open in case someone better comes along. They get to have all the benefits of a wife and none of the responsibility while you play house.

When I was a little girl with my Barbie and Ken dolls, I would make up pretend dates and pretend weddings and pretend homes with them like most little girls. This was all a part of growing up and lots of fun and imagination was involved. It was great to pretend as a child, but now I am a grown woman, and the time for pretending has passed. I don't play house anymore.

Reflections

If he doesn't want what you want, how much of your time are you willing to waste trying to change his mind?

Is it fair to be angry with him when he made himself clear about your relationship, and you disregarded what he said and decided to live in a false reality?

If a man sees you as the woman in his future, should you have to fight to stay the woman in his present?

A man normally takes care of what he values. If you have to fuss and fight to get grocery money, rent money, etc. from someone you're living with, are you of value to him?

Are you happy with what you have settled for?

Are you comfortable with being manipulated? If no, why are you comfortable with being a manipulator?

If it's *just a piece of paper*, why are they working so hard to avoid it? Money is just a piece of paper, but no one tries to avoid possessing it. Is it because they know the value of the *piece of paper*?

As a woman, did you assume the role of the man in your relationship in order to keep the relationship? Are you the provider, the hunter, the stability, and strength? Are you the man?

DAY 13

Your Sexy Can Be Sassy but Trashy Is Never Classy

Almost every woman wants to be attractive to her partner. We usually make a special effort to appeal to the things they find attractive as well as pleasing ourselves. There is nothing wrong with walking in your femininity and accentuating your best assets. Sometimes there is some confusion as to how far this should go.

When a woman presents herself to the world, she should keep in mind how she wants to be perceived. Do you want to be seen as a respectable woman, a woman on the prowl, or an easy lay? Do you want to be seen as a professional in the workplace? Do you want people to assume you are successful so designer labels and bags are important in maintaining your image of success?

The reality of life is people will draw a lot of conclusions about you based on the way you present yourself. Some of these conclusions will be so far from the truth and others will be spot on.

No one can determine what a grown woman can and cannot wear; however, there are a few things you should keep in mind.

Men will treat you the way they perceive you. If a man meets you and your breast, behind, and legs are on full display, he will regard you as sexually available. You have allowed not only him but the general public to see in their full glory some of the most intimate parts of your body. You may think you are being sexy and tell yourself everybody dresses like this. When you walk out your front door exposed to everybody, remember those looking include good men, respectful men, but also criminals, rapists, married men, single men, church folks, children, and everyone else with a set of eyes. Should the person in line behind you at the grocery store know what kind of underwear you are wearing? Are your shorts so short we can see if you have shaved? Will people be motivated to give you the benefit of the doubt in terms of the quality of your character based on your appearance? If you are saying, "I'm grown and I can wear what I want, when I want," you are 100 percent right. But if your outfit is indistinguishable from a $20 hooker walking the street, you may have to defend/protect yourself from being treated like one. That is a real-life consequence of your choices. You are in control of how you present yourself, but you are not now and will not ever be in control of how others will react to you.

Sexy can be beautiful and subtle at the same time. Your guy might think red lipstick is sexy; he may like a certain dress you wear or like your hair down instead of pulled back. Sexy can be coordinating your outfit with his or asking his opinion about what he likes to see you in. His favorite outfit may be your destressed jeans with some heels or a sundress and sandals. When you realize sexy is in the eyes and heart of the beholder, you don't have to or need to go to extremes to catch his eye. My grandmother would always say to us, "There is nothing you can put on or take off that will make you more beautiful than a man's imagination. Leave room for his imagination."

Reflections

Do you realize that when a man cares or loves you, he considers you to be an extension of him?

A man will approach you in accordance with how he perceives you. If he sees you as a lady, he will approach you with respect, but if he sees you as trashy, he will also act accordingly most of the time. How do you want to be approached?

Do you display your body because you think it is all you have to offer?

Do you know when your attire is appropriate or inappropriate for the occasion or environment?

DAY 14

Trying to Change Him Ultimately Changes You

It is not uncommon to have some idea as to the type of man you want in your life. You many want him to be kind, responsible, hard-working, loving, have a great sense of humor, and on and on. The problem is, sometimes we want these things so bad we manufacture them by pretending not to see what is right in front of us.

When he sits next to you on the sofa and gives you that big smile, you think he is the sun and the moon. Then the rain comes and his true character is revealed. He has a track record of irresponsible behavior and denial about the part he plays in his own soap opera-type life.

He has four kids by four women, and he doesn't take care of any of them, but your child is going to be different. He has never kept a job past six months, and it's never his fault. His name has never been on a lease for his own place. He either lives with his momma or his current woman of the hour. He's always available for sex but never to help with repairs or with the household finances. But you love him and he said he loves you, so he's going to change just for you because you are different from every other woman he has ever been with.

He cheated on you, but you tell yourself it wasn't his fault; after all, she threw herself at him and men are weak. Remember when you used to say how you wouldn't stay with a man that cheated on you? Remember, that's what you said when talking to your friend about her cheating boyfriend.

He borrowed money from you and did not pay it back, but he has new tennis shoes or a new PlayStation that he bought instead of paying you back. Two weeks later, you're giving him money again; you even gave him your bill money because you are telling yourself this time will be different. Remember when you used to say you don't understand these women that let a guy use them? You didn't understand these women taking care of grown tail men. You talked about how silly they are, and now look at you. You're in the same boat with one paddle going in circles.

You look at your man, and he is so fine. Body like a Greek god that he got exercising on the yard in prison. But that is his past. He loves you, and he's different now. Just because he gets high four or five times a day or drinks every day doesn't make him a bad guy. I know he hits me sometimes, but that's my fault because he told me to shut up, and I had to say one more thing so it's my fault. He told me he was sorry, and I believed him. He brought me flowers, and we made love.

So it's over; I forgive him. Everybody makes mistakes. Besides, it doesn't happen all the time, and he's always very sweet afterward. "It's going to get better!" she said, giving herself permission to stay in an abusive relationship. It's amazing how much she looks like the same girl that six months ago she was having a conversation about. She didn't understand what would make a woman stay with an abusive or deadbeat man. What a change. A refusal to acknowledge the facts and live in the fantasy has consequences.

> I am not a product of my circumstances; I
> am a product of my decisions. (Steven Covey)

Adults are who they are and where they are because of their choices. We alone are responsible for our choices and our changes.

Reflections

Do you realize you cannot change another adult without their complete cooperation and participation?

Do you realize the more you lie to yourself the easier it will become until you are no longer present in your own reality?

Have you convinced yourself that any man is better than not having a man?

Do you believe in your heart that you deserve more than you have settled for in a man?

DAY 15

I'm Sorry Doesn't Fix Everything

There's a little story I used to tell my students when trying to direct them toward being kinder to their friends. One of the kids was having a birthday, so his mom brought in a birthday cake for him to share with the class. She also brought ice cream cups, and the children were excited at the special treat. Two days earlier, another student had a birthday and for whatever reason, their parents did not bring treats for the class. Well this made Jimmy (not his real name) angry, so he deliberately knocked the cake on the floor and stomped on it. The birthday boy was devastated and began to cry uncontrollably. One of the other kids told Jimmy to say he was sorry because that was not nice. Eventually, he did apologize under pressure from the other kids and he said, "Sorry."

That *sorry* didn't change a thing for the birthday boy. His birthday was still ruined, his cake was still smashed, the other kids still missed their special treat, and all the joy left the room. Even if Jimmy's apology had been sincere, the circumstances were not changed, and the devastation and disappointment were not erased.

Lack of forethought, inconsideration, vengefulness, spite, nasty words, and hurt cannot be erased with an "I'm sorry."

The golden rule still applies: "Do unto others as you would have them do unto you."

I'm sorry has been reduced to *I messed up and somebody saw me, so I'll apologize to put myself back in their good graces.* False regret will never be a deterrent to a repetition of bad behavior.

I'm sorry really is supposed to mean I acknowledge I did something wrong and it hurt you. I regret the pain I've caused you and will, if given another chance, make every effort to not repeat this behavior and cause you further pain.

If when you say I'm sorry that is not what you mean, keep it. If it's not sincere, what you're really saying is, "Get over it cause I'm through dealing with it. You're dismissed because I'm still going to do what I'm going to do." If you are in a relationship of any kind with a person that has no empathy for others and is only concerned with what satisfies their wants or needs, remove yourself and keep a safe distance emotionally.

> An insincere friend is more to be feared than a wild beast; a wild beast may wound your body, but an evil friend will wound your mind. (Buddha)

Reflections

Are your apologies sincere or dismissive?

Have you repeated a behavior that you have previously apologized for? What is your expectation on how many times you should be forgiven?

Did you know what you were doing would hurt that person and you did it anyway to satisfy your wants or needs?

Were you sorry for what you did or sorry you got caught?

DAY 16

Affection is Appreciation, Sex is Gratification

Many of us have seen couples that have been together for years and years, and sometimes we wonder what the secret of such a long relationship could be. If you believe what you see or read, you may believe that good sex is the answer to every question about relationships. One of the things that we don't often talk about is how the bedroom is directly affected by how you treat your partner the rest of the day. Many people are under the impression that affection and sex are the same thing, but they are as different as a cup of juice and a cup of vinegar.

If your relationship has no affection, your sex life will eventually be affected. Ask yourself the question, "Which one of these people would I be most attracted to?"

You wake up in the morning and are greeted by a smiling face and a kiss on your forehead with, "Morning, baby," or "Did you sleep well?" These are your first words of the day. He made a pot of coffee while you were in the shower. He brought you a cup to the bedroom with two spoons of sugar and vanilla creamer because he knows how you like your coffee. While you were doing your makeup, he got the snow off your car and heated it up, so you didn't have to get in a cold car. As you both drove off, he told you not to worry about dinner. He would pick something up, so you could relax this evening.

Now, let's flip the coin on the same situation. You both wake up, but your first words are yelled, "Turn the doggone alarm off, you hear that thing. I have to say the same thing every day." He goes in the kitchen and there's no coffee, so he yells, "Why didn't you make the coffee before you got in the shower?" He starts to make the coffee and realizes you already made it last night; all he had to do was push the button. How are you feeling toward him now? Are your thoughts about making love or getting to work so you can get a break from him? He cleaned his car off but not yours, and as he leaves, he tells you he doesn't want leftovers for dinner today and to make sure you cook when you get home.

Which one of these men will you desire? Desire to please, desire to go the extra step for.

We are more likely to treat people a certain way based on two things—how they treat us and how they make us feel. Affection and consideration for your partner go hand in hand. If your partner feels unappreciated, neglected, taken for granted, and devalued, these feelings will come into your bedroom.

Affection, kindness, and thoughtfulness say to your partner, "I see you and what you do for me, and I appreciate you. I value what you bring to my life. My life is better because of you, and I want to bring these same things from me to you." When a person touches your heart before they touch your body, the dynamics of your physical relationship are substantially improved.

Affection is appreciation, sex is gratification. But understand this—when the two combine in love, then there will be sensual celebration.

Reflections

Is there affection in your relationship without the expectation of sex?

Do you do random acts and receive random acts of kindness and consideration?

Do you know the difference between affection and sex?

DAY 17

It Takes the Same Thing to Keep Him That It Took to Get Him

It's your first date, and you spent the day picking just the right outfit. You got your hair and nails done and have on your best perfume. You want to be as appealing as possible because you really like him and want him to like you. The date goes well, and you go out again and again. You always look fantastic, and now you invite him to dinner. You cook all his favorite things; you fix his plate, refill his drink, and paint this picture of what it would be like if the two of you were to marry. It works, and the two of you are married. You've been married for a good while and now your attitude and efforts to please him have changed. You walk confidently knowing you got him now.

So now the woman who always had her appearance together has gotten really relaxed. You are actually too relaxed; that is, if you are still interested in keeping your appeal with your man. You go to the grocery store or the mall with him in pajamas or dirty clothes and house shoes. If he was to run into a friend or coworker, he could be embarrassed to even introduce you as his wife. You are not representing him as a wife that has a husband she cares about or a husband that takes care of his wife and family. You look thrown away, lazy, and depressed. When he comes home now, your hair hasn't been combed, there is food spilled on your shirt, and your feet are dirty because you have not bathed. You called him and said bring home some chicken because you didn't feel like cooking.

There should be no expectation that you will be dressed up at all times, but cleanliness and proper grooming are not an unreasonable expectation. You no longer cook anything he likes, but now only cook what you and the kids like. He'll be all right; what he gonna do? He's lucky I cooked at all. This is the same man that you catered to when you were trying to hook him. You won't do for him what he sees you do for you girlfriends. When you go somewhere with them, you spend two days picking your outfit, and you make sure your hair is together. But with your husband, you look like something the cat dragged in. This is not how you started this relationship. This makes you either a liar because you falsely misrepresented who you are or a manipulator because you led him to believe he was in a relationship with someone that wanted him to be a priority in their life.

Your husband married a liar. You painted a picture of a life with you that you had no intention of maintaining. You set a trap to capture your prey, and now that it's caught, you are falsely under the impression there are no other hunters watching and waiting. You saw his potential, so did she. You know he's a good man, so does she. He was a priority, and now he's an afterthought.

My mom said to me more than a few times, "Some men go out and cheat, others are sent."

I didn't understand this immediately. I thought she was justifying a man cheating, but she wasn't. She was saying three things:

1. The same thing it took to get him, it takes to keep him.
2. A man should not have to leave home because he's not getting what you promised at home.
3. A person is far more likely to stay put where they are valued and appreciated.
   She was married forty-five years before her death.

Don't start what you're not willing to continue.

If you married a man who was working forty hours or more a week, helps keep the bills paid, keeps your car in tip-top shape, and one day it all just stopped, how would you feel? Instead of hitting the floor every morning to go to work, he says he doesn't want to work anymore; it's too much trouble. He says you need to get another job, so you can pay more of the bills. If your car is down, he decides it's too hot or too cold to fix it. Catch the bus; he'll do it later, but he just doesn't feel like it right now.

Are your feelings the same about something being too much of an effort when you are on the receiving end of being an afterthought? When your position is changed from priority to afterthought, from number one to around number sixteen, does it make you want to stay with or stray from that person? I repeat—you saw he was a good man, so did she. Don't give an opening, being overconfident to the point of neglecting your mate. You are not the only hunter.

Reflections

If your attitude toward him was also his attitude toward you, how would you feel?

If proper hygiene is too much of an effort to maintain yourself for your husband, why should he want to be with you physically or emotionally?

Are you leaving or making an opening for another woman to fill the voids you are leaving in your relationship?

Have you gotten too comfortable or lazy about working to maintain your relationship?

DAY 18

A Parent Is a Role Model. What Are You Modeling?

Once you give birth to a child and decide to raise him or her, you become a role model for that child. It does not matter what the circumstances of that birth may have been. You may have been married or single, the pregnancy may have been planned or unplanned, you may be financially prepared for that child or in the struggle to provide. It does not matter and will not change the fact that you are a role model, and what you do in front of the child will alter their life either for the better or for the worse.

Many years ago, when I was a child and adults gathered together and had adult conversation, children were sent from the room. It was commonly understood that young children were not mature enough to be privy to adult topics of conversation. Children today are exposed to things that innocent and impressionable children should not have any knowledge of at such a young age. Five-year-old children should not know about oral sex, cocaine, all the different names for weed, how to role a joint, or who is *knocking boots* in the neighborhood from listening to your adult conversations and so much more. Seven- or eight-year-olds should not know saying someone "got to do a dime" means they got ten years in prison. Let them be children while they can.

Now it's at this point someone is saying you can't tell me how to raise my child, and once again, you are correct.

I can only give you some insight to the consequences of some of the choices and the impact they have on children.

I stated before that I worked in education for twenty-seven years and before that another six years in social services. I am speaking not about what I heard but what I've seen with my own eyes. I have to admit, I've had my heart broken and cried many tears because of the lost innocence of children far too soon.

Have you done drugs in front of your child? Somebody has because I've seen them roll toilet paper like it's a joint and pretend they are getting high.

Have you had sex in front or your children or left the bedroom door open or let them hear you during sex?

Somebody has because they simulate sex acts on their classmates as early as preschool, and by second grade, they are writing notes to each other with promises of sex acts if you'll be their boyfriend or girlfriend, check yes or no.

Do they hear you talking to your girlfriend about how you are going to "give her some" so she will get your feet and nails done? Well now they think it's okay to trade a kiss for some of their friend's candy. It's what you taught them by example—to trade their body for stuff.

There is a quote by an unknown author that says, "Children may not hear what you say, but they never fail to see what you do."

Let me give you a few questions just as food for thought. If you answer honestly, would you be proud of the example you are setting as your child's first and most important role model?

1. How many men have you let "live with" you?
2. How much exposure does your child have to your sex life? Porn?
3. Does your child know and see you or friends do drugs?
4. Have you brought criminal activity or allowed criminal activity in your home with your children?

5. Have your kids ever seen you hold down a job, or is welfare and food stamps their only example?
6. Are you feeding a man who contributes nothing and running short of food for your children?
7. Are you supporting a grown man so you don't have to be by yourself?
8. Are you allowing your children to see you verbally or physically abused?

You know and I know these questions could go on forever. The point is your child will develop a mindset, a way of thinking that is directly related to what you expose them to.

If you are constantly calling a child stupid or dumb, *they will believe you and give up on themselves. They will see themselves as inferior to others and a disappointment to you. They will not feel loved. When children don't feel loved, they become angry. When children become angry, they become problems and often dangerous to society.*

Women will often end up in relationships with men that will only use them just because they don't want to be alone. They substitute sex for love because no one has taught them the difference.

Parenting is serious. Bad parenting can change all of society. No matter how cute you dress your child or what kind of expensive tennis shoes or gaming systems you buy them, this will not make them a successful or happy person. They will outgrow the shoes and clothes; they will get bored with whatever new toy you buy, but quality of character will remain if taught properly. Self-worth will remain if taught properly.

Homework teaches a work ethic—work then play. You are fighting with your child's teacher because you don't want to be bothered with it and want the responsibility for the education to be the complete responsibility of the teacher. This isn't every parent but yet far too many.

Getting to school on time teaches punctuality for the job. We often form our adult habits in childhood.

Putting their toys away teaches that you are responsible for your own messes. You will be surprised how the amount of mess decreases when you have to be the one that cleans up what you messed up.

Please and *thank you* are expressions of gratitude for the things people do for you that they don't have to do. Children with manners have been taught this; it is a life skill. Rudeness provokes people and that's how many fights start.

Parenting is serious. Dysfunctional children become dysfunctional adults.

Doing things the right way is always less painful than having to make corrections. Be a parent that's friendly, not a friend that happens to be your parent. They'll have lots of friends, but only two, sometimes one, active parent.

Reflections

If you don't want your child to grow up to do it as a teenager or adult, why are you modeling the behavior?

Why are you yelling at your little girl about being "fast or boy crazy" at seven years old, but you are living with the fifth man since she was born? Don't model the behavior.

Why are you yelling at your child for doing drugs or smoking weed when they stole it from your stash? Don't model the behavior.

Why are you angry and yelling at your adult children needing to get a job when they have never seen you hit a clock or any of your boyfriends? Don't model the behavior.

DAY 19

You Need Life Skills so You Can Handle Your Business

When we become adults, the things we have to handle to keep life running smoothly are vastly different than that carefree life when Mom and Dad handled everything. When you are a kid, you don't have to worry about bills, groceries, home repairs, balancing the checkbook, and so on and so on. It's a list that seem to be without end.

When you get your first job, you begin spending the money on all those things you want but your parents wouldn't or couldn't buy. At sixteen, you don't worry about the electric bill because every time you hit the light switch, the light comes on. You don't worry about if is there something in the house to eat because Momma goes to the grocery store every Saturday. As children, we take our comforts for granted because all the efforts to keep us comfortable are the responsibility of someone else, your parents.

Life as an adult changes all of these. Now it's on you to provide your own food, pay your own bills, provide your own shelter, and manage your own money. You have to become a problem solver. What do I do when I have $500 but $600 worth of bills? You can't opt out of things anymore just because they are not fun and are unpleasant. You have all these adult responsibilities that if you don't meet them have severe consequences.

If you buy shoes instead of paying the light bill, you'll wear them in the dark. Didn't pay your gas bill, hope those pipes don't freeze, and the electric heater doesn't cause a fire or burn anybody.

Life skills are necessary for a successful adult life. Cute and sassy won't take care of business. I asked a coworker once what she was making for dinner and she responded, "The only thing I make for dinner is reservations." She was so proud of the fact that she couldn't cook. She was a twenty-eight-year-old woman that didn't have enough survival life skills to be able to put a meal on the table. I love a good restaurant, but as an adult, what happens when the money is low, and you can't prepare a balanced meal for your children or your husband because you can't cook? You don't have to be a five star chef, but basic meals should be doable.

Can you make a household budget and stick to it at least most of the time? Have you ever been educated about what should be priority with the money once you get paid?

What kind of credit score do you have, and do you know what a credit score is and how it affects your buying power?

Can you balance your checkbook, do the laundry, fill out an application for employment, give a good interview, and use grammatically correct language when necessary? I remember one summer when working with training high school students on how to complete an application and interview for a job. How horribly shocked I was with some of the answers on the mock applications. In the space where it asked the sex of the applicant, a few replied yes, meaning yes, I do have sex. When asked why you should be considered for the job, several of them replied, "I don't know" or "I just want a job, so I can buy me some nice stuff." Applying for a job is a vitally necessary life skill.

These are just some of the responsibilities of adulthood. How are you measuring up? Do you even realize when you buy a car with bad credit you may pay 17 to 20 percent interest, but with good credit, you may pay 2 to 6 percent interest? Do you realize bad credit cost you thousands and thousands of dollars over your lifetime?

You need to understand that if you handle adult responsibilities like a child, you will still suffer adult consequences.

Remember the old saying is true, "Those that fail to plan are planning to fail." Adults have to think ahead, plan ahead, and use their head. You cannot plan your future on the sweat and labor of another person. It is your responsibility to carry your own load. You are responsible for your own meat and potatoes, housing yourself, clothing yourself, and being accountable for yourself.

Everybody has needed or will need help sometimes, but this should not be your norm. No one wants to be around someone that always has their hand out begging or wanting you to clean up the mess they made. The problem with people that have no discipline about life skills is they want your money but not your advice. Food for thought: You might want to listen to the advice of the person that's in a position to handle all their needs and wants with enough leftover that they can still help you. They are doing something right that you need to learn how to do.

Reflections

How often have you had to be bailed out of a financial mess you created with your choices?

Do you have a savings for emergencies? Can you get a signature loan if you need to in a pinch?

Do you have to have a cosigner before making a major purchase?

Are you living above your means?

Do you spend your money on what you want and depend on someone else to supply what you need?

DAY 20

Progress is Uncomfortable, It Requires Change

I hate my job, but I won't look for another one. I've got ten years invested with this company, and it's better than nothing. One day I'm going to leave and work someplace else. I've been shacked up with my boyfriend for years. I really want to be married, but I don't want to lose him. Yeah, I know I settled for shacking up and time keeps passing. I know I'm getting older, and I've had three kids by him and it's not what I want. But it's been so long and I'm just used to him; it was comfortable even if it's not really what I want.

I'm going to start going to church when I get my life right, but girl, when Sunday rolls around that bed has a hold on me and it's so comfortable. I'll go next time.

There are people that will have a pair of comfortable shoes that they are so attached to that they continue to wear way too long. There is a hole in the sole, the heal is run over, and the leather is worn and shredded.

This is a metaphor for holding on to what's comfortable for too long.

The hole in the bottom means although you are comfortable, your protection against things that will hurt you is gone.

The worn and laid over heel will twist your foot out of alignment the same way you will contort and distort your thinking to justify staying with the familiar and comfortable.

The shredded and torn leather signifies how things are falling apart, but you still won't let go and move on to a new level of comfort that will protect you, will support you, and will hold it together, allowing you to keep moving forward. Coming out of that old shoe has been so comfortable and allowed yourself to move forward without the fear. Is this the day it all falls apart because I would not change? I would not change my job, my patterns in relationships, my comfort zone. Refusing to change can become a stumbling block to your potential.

Are you allowing staying comfortable to impede you making progress and moving into a more positive direction?

You have a choice in how you choose to live your life. Will you strive to live your best life and be your best self, or will you continue to wear the raggedy shoes? With each step you become more frustrated about your lack of progress and your lack of hope for a better and brighter future because you won't leave your comfort zone. Maybe today you will decide you deserve better than what you have settled for and support yourself, protect yourself, and start walking toward a more fulfilled life.

I once worked with a woman who every day wore a pair of plain black pumps to work. Winter, spring, summer, and fall, she wore those pumps. One weekend, she broke her ankle, so she was forced to wear a flat shoe on that foot. I'm not even making this up, I promise. She was so stuck in her comfort zone with those black pumps that she wore one black pump and a white tennis shoe on the other foot. Two different heel heights which gave her a limp but to her it made sense. She did not realize what a prisoner she was to her own habits and comfort zone.

If you refuse to venture outside your comfort zone and risk being a little uncomfortable, you are making a life choice. Only you can decide whether you will spend your life walking forward or limping along.

Reflections

When is the last time you tried something new?

Are you working a job you hate because you've gotten comfortable?

Are you in a relationship that brings you no joy but you've gotten comfortable for fear of being alone?

If you keep doing the same thing over and over again and it's not working for you, why do you keep doing it that way?

DAY 21

Stop Whitewashing Red Flags, Pink Is Not the True Color

Inside every person is a built-in warning system. It is there for our protection and direction. This warning system alerts us of hidden dangers, so we can make the necessary adjustments for our protection. Some people call it an inner voice; others call it the Holy Spirit or God's voice.

Your body will react physically to these warnings by an increased heart rate, rapid breathing, and an inability to calm yourself and relax. Mentally you will have a heightened sense of awareness about your surroundings and the people or person currently in your space.

When these alerts or alarms go off, you have to decide how you will respond. You have the option of taking the necessary steps to protect yourself and deal with the situation with honesty. You have to recognize it is what it is and not what you want it to be. But like most things in life, this is not the only option. You also can choose to distort the truth and whitewash all the red flags by disguising them as pink. You will tell yourself, "Well, that's not really what he meant to say" or "He only hit me that one time." You'll say, "He stole my ATM card, but he said he was sorry." You know he has never had his own apartment or kept a job for over six months, but it's because they were picking on him.

He wants to take care of all his kids, but their moms be tripping because they want him back.

Do you find yourself making more excuses for him than he even makes for himself? Do you justify all of his wrongdoings? Do you help him cover up the lies and the things he has done to hurt those that trusted him? You are a whitewasher of facts and reality. You are painting red alarms with what you'll call white lies. You do this so you can tell yourself it's not red, it's pink. Pink is a soft, gentle color. Red is bold and bright to get your attention. It warns you to stop and assess before continuing to move ahead. Don't let your whitewashing leave you bleeding your red blood. Life doesn't always afford you a second chance; whitewashing can cost you your life.

Reflections

Has ignoring a red flag ever put you in danger?

Do you find ways to justify when you are being mistreated?

Have friends or family been put in dangerous situations in an effort to protect you?

Have you ignored that inner voice that was warning you to leave the situation? But you ignored it, and later paid a price for this decision? What did you learn, or did you learn anything?

DAY 22

No One Rushes Home to Nagging Nancy or Arguing Angela

Have you ever gotten up in a pretty good mood, you dress for work, the drive-in is clear with no delays, and you're feeling calm and at peace? You walk over to your work space and before you can take off your coat and put your purse away, here comes that one person who throws everything off into another direction.

Let me paint the scene. You've got one arm in your coat and one arm out, and you're being bombarded.

"I thought you would be here ten minutes ago. Did you do that report I said I needed? What are you going to do about the supplies we need? You need to order more supplies. We're always running out of something. That other office never runs out. I guess whoever orders their supplies knows what they're doing."

This laundry list of complaints and demands can go on for quite a while, and your entire mood has been changed. You were feeling pretty good until you got bum-rushed before you could even get you coat off.

Now I want you to do a role reversal. Imagine this same dynamic if you were greeted like this and you had a bad morning.

Are you guilty of being a joy crusher for others, for your husband? When he comes home from work, are you complaining about the kids, the house, your car, and the bills before he can even take his coat off? Is there even one of these complaints that couldn't have waited maybe for one hour? Did you take the time to welcome him home or appreciate him? Did you allow time to unwind, shake off the trails of the day, before you attacked?

Let me say to all the women reading this—I recognize that many of you are in the same position as he is. You work all day and have to come home and cook, deal with the kids, and clean house. Where is your hour to unwind and shake off the day? I'm glad you asked; your unwind time is in how you inspired him to take care of your needs because you're taking care of him. Your break is in the motivation he has to keep you happy because he sees you acknowledging he's working to be a good provider in partnership with you. You are letting him know his contribution lightens your load because you are not carrying all this responsibility alone. His thank you may be bringing dinner home or ordering pizza, so you don't have to cook. Maybe he will start cooking sometimes or throw in a load of laundry or two to help lighten your load. He may take the kids to the movies, so you can take a nap. Appreciation and consideration usually inspires the same toward the one who is showing you these qualities. One hand washes the other. They work in cooperation with one another to get the job done.

The point here is this: no one wants to come home to yelling, nagging, and complaints every day. This is especially true as soon as you walk in the door. Both the man and the woman want to be appreciated and have their contributions to the home recognized and acknowledged. Home should be a refuge from the hardships of everyday life. Greet your mate (men and women) the way you would like to be greeted as you enter your home. Home is not only where the heart is, it should also be the place where you can unwind and have a level of peace the world doesn't offer. Unfortunately, we live in a world of me, me, me instead of we, we, we. Greet the way you want to be greeted. Appreciate the way you want to be appreciated.

Put into your relationship the things you would like to receive.

Reflections

How eager would you be to walk through a door if you know on the other side of it is nagging, complaining, and arguing?

Is there peace, harmony, and cooperation in your home?

Would you want to come home to you?

Is your home a place where you feel love and give love, or is there always a battle going on?

DAY 23

God Forgives, Sometimes People, Not So Much

Many times in our lives when we become angry or feel like someone has wronged us, we want to get even. We want to make them hurt the way they made us hurt but more so. It's the old you're-kicked-by-dog-so-I-kicked-your cat mindset. You will even hear people incorrectly quote the Bible by saying that it says an eye for an eye. In actuality, it says seek not an eye for an eye. It actually says, "Vengeance is mine, says the Lord."

In an ideal world, we would not spend valuable time plotting and scheming against those we are angry with. This vengefulness takes many forms. You may have seen car windows being broken, tires slashed, calls to wives from mistresses, unreasonable alimony and child support request, using children as weapons against one another, and so on and so forth. You may justify these actions because you're mad and you want to strike out. You want them to be upset and to have their life disrupted because yours is. You tell the kids their daddy isn't about anything, and he's a dog. He tells the kids you were a whore, and they might not even be his child. The goal is not to move forward to your best life but to win the war you have waged against another person. This war can go on for years and years.

You will not let them have the last word or have peace because you're mad, and you have decided to make their life a living hell. You are never going to forgive them or yourself for even getting in this situation. You should have known he was a bum and no good.

You need to learn the art of forgiveness. Until you forgive, you can't move on with your life. You will always compare everybody that comes behind him to him. You need to unpack the anger, the resentment, and that vengeful nature and live your best life in peace.

If you are saying you can't forgive them, then they own you. While you're steaming, they have gone on with their life. You're bad-mouthing him to your friends, and they are telling him everything you say while they laugh at you.

Forgiveness doesn't mean you have to be friends or hang out. Forgiveness doesn't mean you have to give them an opportunity to hurt you again or even trust them again. Forgiveness means I will no longer give you a space in my thoughts and my decisions that keep me from being at peace and moving forward. Forgiveness releases the anger that is triggered every time you relive what happened. Forgiveness allows you to learn from what happened, so you don't repeat the same mistake. Forgiveness allows you to admit the part you played in all the drama, so you can move on.

You also have done things that required someone to forgive you, and you wanted them to extend you that understanding and grace. You cannot ask of others things you are not willing to give. The Lord's Prayer says, "Forgive us our trespasses *as we forgive those who trespassed against us...*" Don't cut yourself off from forgiveness in your determination to hold a grudge and get even. The price of unforgiveness is too high and can block a blessing you are too angry to receive.

Reflections

Do you realize if you remain angry and unforgiving toward the old man, you leave no room for the new one? Don't block your blessing.

What have you done that required someone to have to forgive you?

How can you ask of others something you are unable or unwilling to give in return?

Are your children paying the price of your unforgiveness?

DAY 24

Minnie the Moocher and Glenda Get Over Are Sisters

Recently on Facebook, there was a post from a young man taking a poll about a situation that happened to him on a first date. Here are the particulars. He took this young woman to dinner at this particular restaurant; they had friendly conversation, finished their dinner, and as they were preparing to leave, she asked him to buy two additional dinners for her to take home to her children. He refused, and so the rest of the evening she had an attitude with him. She became snappy and borderline nasty in her responses because he refused to buy her children dinner. His question to the general public was, "Did I do something wrong, or should I have bought the dinners?"

This is a prime example of Minnie the Moocher aka Glenda Get Over. This is the first time you've ever been on a date with this man, and you're actively trying to get everything you can as fast as you can. Your actions have told this man so much about you in one date it's almost unbelievable. First, if you are telling the truth about your kids being hungry, it means you left to go on a date without feeding your own kids. It also means you went depending on his being so strung out on you that you would be able to manipulate him into doing whatever you wanted. You also let him know you will eat even when your kids have not. You have let him know you don't take care of business because if the kids are hungry, you must not have

91

food in the house or I assume you would have fed them. By the way, who is caring for them that they won't feed hungry kids?

Now to put the icing on the cake, now you have an attitude because you are under the very false impression that somebody owes you something. Those are not his children but yours. There is no established relationship or commitment between the two of you whereby he has accepted you and your children are a package deal. It's a first date.

The problem with a moocher is they are always looking for an opportunity to get over. Every person is a potential target in their efforts to get something for nothing. Now when the plan doesn't work, you get to see the other side of them. Maybe they'll curse you out, give you attitude, threaten to end the relationship, or make a scene. They are people that have a goal of getting as much as they can while doing as little as they can.

People with a user mentality don't care about the lengths they have to go to. They don't care how their use of you impacts your life or circumstances. They are not worried about hurting you. In order to be a successful moocher, you must be a liar and without conscience. You must have a comfort level with taking advantage of others.

Moochers and those who are constantly trying to get over will use friends, family, strangers, and children. They will tell themselves this makes them clever and totally absolve themselves of any responsibility. They will say to themselves you are stupid, or you didn't have to do what they asked you to do. You loaned them money, but they never paid it back. You let them move in, and they stole from you. You agreed to watch their children for two hours; they didn't come back until the next day. You let them use your car; they brought it back with no gas in it. Everyone they come in contact with they use and use until the person drops them. The moocher will then go around telling others what a fool you were rather than what a friend you were.

A moocher will never put your needs before theirs.

Their apologies are just used to reopen a door you may have closed to them. It means you caught them in their lie, but they want a chance to use you again.

Users come male and female. Moochers avoid responsibility and always have an excuse for their actions.

Moochers and freeloaders are the same thing—a person looking to survive and thrive at someone else's expense and someone else's labor. Remember that ladies when he wants to move in and you will be the fourth or fifth woman he has lived with. This doesn't include all the times he moved back to his momma's house in between women.

If you want to shut down a moocher, let me give you the only tool that works. When they ask for the fruits of your labor say, "No!" and stick to it with, no explanation. Just NO! You do not owe anyone an explanation on how you allocate the resources/money you have earned by hitting the floor each day and working for what you need and want.

Reflections

If they don't care enough about themselves to work to take care of their own needs, why would you think they care about you?

If they burned you once and then burned you again, why do you keep handing them a new book of matches?

Did anything in their past warn you that they would not keep their promise to you or honor the debt and you ignored it?

Are you making loans that prevent you from being able to fulfill your own responsibilities? Ex: You loaned out your rent money; they didn't pay you back, and now you can't pay your rent.

DAY 25

Anybody Is Not Better Than Nobody

Many times, when a woman has become weary or tired of waiting for Mr. Right, she will begin to allow negative men and relationships into her life. Mr. Right is nowhere to be found, so I'll settle for Mr. Right Now, Mr. It's Just Something to Do, or Mr. Better Than Nothing.

Settling for Mr. Better Than Nothing will bring more drama, heartbreak, and turmoil to your life than you can even imagine. These men have very long track records of leaving a trail of misery behind. This misery will manifest itself in many ways. When we enter these relationships, we see the warnings. Many times, we have heard about the way they operate ahead of time, but we ignore what we see and what we've been told. We don't want to be alone, so we take a chance on him. We tell ourselves that we are so special things will be different with us. We make excuses and blame the women that they were involved with saying, "She just didn't know how to keep her man happy." We will tell ourselves whatever we have to in order to justify our choices. We invite a dysfunctional, whorish, dope-dealing-and-using alcoholic, abusive, having-no-job, deadbeat dad with seven baby mommas and a criminal record longer that Highway 70 into our lives and the lives of our children. Your reward for that is you get to say you got somebody.

You're taking care of him but he's the man.

He eats all the food that you cook for him, but he doesn't buy any groceries but he's the man.

He drives your car and wrecked it but didn't get it fixed, but he's the man.

He cheats with other women and stays out all night, but he came back home cause he's your man.

He's abusive and embarrasses you in front of others, but he's the man.

He doesn't help you pay a single bill, but he enjoys every comfort of your house that you enjoy but he's the man.

He is the man, he is the man. He is the man you let use you. He is the man you let abuse you. He is the man you let drain you, disrespect you, and he is the man you settle for, so you wouldn't be alone. He is also the man that you are parading in front of your child or children as an example of what it means to be a man.

Is this the type of man you would want for your daughter to date? Is this the type of man you would want your son to grow up to be? Children will imitate your behavior and the standards you put in place because it becomes the norm for them.

Mr. Anybody may beat you, steal from you, molest your children, and any number of other nasty and dangerous things. Many have died at the hands of Mr. Better Than Nothing or Mr. That Will Do for Now.

Spend some time nurturing yourself, so you can move forward knowing you deserve better.

If you were thirsty and asked me for water and I served it to you in a really dirty glass, you would reject the water. You want to quench your thirst, but you don't want the filth that I'm serving up with the water.

Why would you not accept the water you want to quench your thirst because the glass is dirty, but you'll accept a man covered in the filth of his choices just because you're thirsty for a man?

Reflections

When did you decide you don't deserve a good man?

When did you decide you were so unappealing and unworthy that you have to settle for anybody?

What is your biggest fear about having some time alone without a partner?

What example are you setting for your children?

Is Mr. Anybody a danger to you or your children?

DAY 26

It's More Than Okay to Say No, It's Your Right

One of the things my mom used to tell me is to protect your reputation because once you lose it, you never get it back. She used as an example when she attended her fortieth high school reunion. There was a classmate there that in high school had a reputation for sleeping around with many boys. While at the reunion forty years later, there was a group of men talking about her. They were discussing how many of them had sex with her and what she did. Her reputation was still following her forty years later. Forty years later, she was still being described as a whorish woman that everybody had a piece of. She may have completely turned her life around, but her reputation is what people still remember about her.

There are going to be times when a man may ask you to do things *just for him* that can come back and bite you in the butt when you least expect it.

Has he asked you to take nude pictures, make a pornographic video, engage in a threesome, or maybe have sex in public with some kind of thrill of getting caught? Has he asked you to do drugs to increase the intensity of sex?

Well, what happens when the relationship doesn't work out and things get ugly? Will those *just-for-him* pictures now get put on social media? Will he send copies to your parents and friends? Will he post them in the bathroom at your school? Will he just tell everyone you know the things he got you to do to destroy your reputation?

Angry people, hurt people, and vindictive people will strike out to retaliate for whatever wrong they think you committed against them. Sometimes they will strike out as a means of trying to control you.

Unfortunately, many people live to get the dirt on others, and they spread that dirt like salt on a snowy sidewalk. The intention is the same as that salt—to break you down, so they can walk all over you.

Protect your reputation because once it's gone, you can't get it back. That decision you made today to accommodate someone else's fantasy could become a stranglehold or a weapon that could be used against you for years and years to come.

When people are angry, boastful, or vindictive, they will often do things that satisfy their need to get even with no regard for how it will change someone's life long-term if not forever.

Do not give people damaging images or information to use against you. Consider this—if a person has your best interest at heart and truly wants what is best for you, would they even have asked you to participate in some of these activities? Imagine a porno tape being sent to your job or your church. Imagine nude pictures being posted in the men's restroom at your school. These things happen in real life. If you don't think before you act, you will eventually reap the consequences of your bad choices.

Reflections

What is your reputation with the people in your past and your present?

Why were you so easily convinced into these activities?

Did you think if you said yes this would sustain the relationship?

Where you afraid if you didn't make the video or take the pictures you would be replaced by someone who would comply?

If you did everything he asked and he still cheated or left you for someone else, what are you left with?

DAY 27

The Alphabet Has 26 Letters They Are All Letters but Each of Them, Like Men, Is Different

One of the things we must acknowledge as women is that all men are not the same. When you believe all men are the same, you will never be able to see the man in front of you. You will only see the man or men from your past. You believe if that one hurt you so will this because they are all the same. That one cheated on you, and all men are cheaters so this will, too; it's just a matter of time.

I have heard women apply this type of logic to men, but let's change the dynamics of the situation and apply this logic to ourselves.

Your sister stole $5 out of your mom's purse, so your mom spanked you because all kids are the same.

Your coworker comes to work every day twenty minutes late, so your boss docks your check because all employees are the same.

Your man's ex got pregnant by another man, so he puts a tracker on your phone and car. He won't allow you to have a conversation with any male because all women are the same.

Women will often make these general statements out of hurt. You didn't resolve the situation with the person that did hurt you, so you're punishing the person that hasn't done anything wrong.

Have you decided he's guilty before the situation has even happened? I ask because once we decide in our mind a person is guilty, our attitude changes. We begin to be suspicious of everything. You want to know who's on the phone every time it rings. We want to know why he was fifteen minutes late getting home from work. Why do you have to take a shower as soon as you get home? These behaviors are the result of distrust of all men because of the actions of someone from your past. That someone has absolutely nothing to do with the person standing in front of you.

Thinking and believing that all men are the same will cost you potentially great relationships. You have built a barrier to try to prevent being hurt again. There is nothing wrong in being cautious but not so cautious that you prevent yourself from moving forward.

One of the ways you can move forward is to acknowledge the hurt instead of acting like having your heart broken didn't impact you. Forgive, but take the time to evaluate what went wrong and when. What was your part? Did you ignore the red flags warning you this person was not who they pretended to be? You may also need to evaluate whether it was him or it was you that was the problem. You cannot learn if you can't be honest with yourself. That is like walking down the same street over and over and expecting to arrive at a different location.

You cannot start the next chapter of your life if you keep rereading the last one. Turn the page.

Reflections

If you have to stalk him, check his phone and social media, which one are you—jealous, distrustful, or have low self-esteem? Maybe all of the above.

Do you want to pay for what the women of his past did or be seen as an individual with your own qualities?

Are you looking for a real man with good character and qualities but not perfect, or are you looking for some fantasy of a perfect man you've created in your head?

Do you have the qualities in you that you are trying to find in him?

DAY 28

You Can Buy a Boy but You Can't Buy a Man

Occasionally, I find myself watching some of the Court TV programming, and there is a very, very common case that keeps appearing over and over.

Boy meets girl, boy and girl engage in sexual activity, girl begins to spend or loan or give large sums of money to boy. The terms of this exchange of money changes based on the current dynamics of the relationship.

If everything is going great, the money was a gift because I love you and what's mine is yours.

If things are shaky or in turmoil, then the money was a loan and was given with an expectation of securing your position or encouraging the person to stick with you because look at all that I do for you. You owe me commitment and fidelity.

If the relationship doesn't work out, then the money was definitely only a loan, and you didn't do right by me so now, I want my money back, *right now*! You want to be with her? Let her pay your car note, buy you expensive tennis shoes, or designer clothes. I want my money back.

In all of these *situationships*, the money was a tool as much as a hammer is to a nail.

The money was the tool of obligation—you owe me.

The money was the tool of security—I know he's not going anywhere because nobody's going to do for him all the things I do.

Girl, he will take your money and spend it on the woman he really does actually like.

The money is the tool of revenge—you didn't obey me and do what I wanted, so you must be punished. Give me back all my toys, I'm burning the clothes, and taking you to court to get my money back. You won't wear the clothes I bought you looking good on my dime with some other woman.

Ladies, let me make it clear in plain English. Money will only allow you to rent a boy for a period of time until he gets a better offer. *You cannot buy love no matter how much money you spend. You can only rent some time.*

These are little boys walking around masquerading as men. They are looking to be taken care of with the fringe benefit of sex. They look like men, they smell like men, but they don't walk in the shoes of manhood.

When a man enters a relationship, he seeks to bring something to the table. If you constantly cook for him, he'll start buying the groceries. If he uses your car, he will put gas in it before returning it to you.

A man has his own place and has maintained his own place for a significant period of time. He has his own credit and can sign his own name to purchase the things he needs just like you should be able to do. A man has a job. Let me repeat that—he has a job or is retired from a job and has his own source of *legal* and *steady* income. He is a source of help to you as you are to him.

If you are housing, feeding, and dressing your "man," he is not your man, he is your dependent just like your child.

Men will commit their money to anything and anyone they want to secure as part of their life. If he is not investing in you, it might be because you're just not that important to him. A man will buy the best car wax and spend two or three hours detailing his car because he loves it, but he can't take you to the grocery store or help you paint a room. He only has time to do with you the things he wants to do with you.

If his hand is always extended to you empty but when he draws it back it's full, you are not his woman; he is your pimp. You work for him, and in all probability you're not the only one.

You can buy and/or rent a boy, but you cannot buy and/or rent a man. A man knows the importance of walking in a man's role in the home, in the relationship, and in life.

Money's only purpose is to purchase things, not people and not affection.

Ask yourself, "Why are you so insecure and unaware of your own value that you would pay someone to spend time with you?"

He didn't play you; you played yourself.

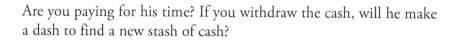

Reflections

Are you paying for his time? If you withdraw the cash, will he make a dash to find a new stash of cash?

Are your kids doing well without the things they need while you're taking care of his needs?

Why is he waiting on your check, payday, income tax return, or any other form of income like his name is on it? Why does he know how much your source of income is each month?

What do you call a woman who sleeps with a man for cash? Did you say prostitute? Why is it different when it's him?

DAY 29

Don't Quit in the Battle
Put on Your Armor, and Fight for Your Life!

If you have read all the previous chapters and have made it to this point in the book, you have no doubt at some point that some of your past behaviors were called out. Maybe you have been enlightened to a new way of seeing the truth in various situations. Maybe you've been made aware the part you have played in some of the drama and tragedies of your life. My goal here is to empower you and help you live your best life.

As women, every day we will encounter something or someone that will try to make us feel inadequate. Sometimes these messages will be directly in our face, and other times, they will be implied and subliminal.

You will be told you're not pretty enough, smart enough, educated enough, sophisticated enough, sexy enough, or successful enough. Values will be assigned to your self-worth based on what kind of job you have, how much you weigh, what neighborhood you live in, or what you wear and look like.

If you let the thoughts, words, and actions of others define you, defeat is inevitable.

If you do not make up in your own mind your value or worth, I promise you, your life will become flooded with people who will make the decision for you.

As a mother, sister, and aunt, if someone were verbally attacking your loved one, calling them stupid, worthless, a good-for-nothing piece of trash, you would defend, protect, and do battle to protect them. Why would you not protect yourself with the same amount of energy and determination? Are you less important, less valuable, or less worthy of being respected? Do you not deserve to be treated kindly?

Ladies, we are responsible for the things we allow others to bring into our lives. *It is not your job to change their behavior; it is your job to keep that behavior away from you.*

In this world, there are predators everywhere waiting to pounce. They are experts at identifying those that have low self-esteem and need the approval of others to feel valued.

We call these predators by many names.

The con man that talked you out of your money with the promise of paying you back then disappeared.

The pimp that talked so sweetly, got you to trust him, then put you on the street.

The player who talked his way into your heart and your house but pays no or very little bills and doesn't support you or his children.

The criminal that has every excuse known to man why he's not going to work on some low-wage job when he can make ten times that *handling his business on the street.*

The liar who never owns up to any of their behaviors and always claims, whenever something goes wrong, it wasn't their fault. She lied on me, they lied on me, or it wasn't even like that.

The married man whose wife just doesn't understand him, and he's going to leave her, just not yet, the time isn't right.

This list could go on and on.

In every person, there is a will to survive that we are born with. It is there to strengthen us to fight for our lives. In order to fight, you have to first believe you are worth fighting for regardless of the mistakes you've made in the past.

Each day provides a new opportunity to make a change for the better. It's a new chance to forgive yourself and move forward down a better path into your future. You cannot do this holding on to the mistakes of your past. Learn from your past mistakes by examining them, gathering all the information, and turning it into a lesson, not a prison. You can't get past or be released from the mistakes of your past if you cannot be honest with yourself. The are no shortcuts; you have to walk it out like a grown woman. Unlock the lesson and walk toward the freedom of another chance to get it right.

Life is a series of experiences all designed to make us better, stronger, and wiser.

When you are fighting for your best life, take the steps toward victory in the battle.

Strive to be better than you were yesterday.

Build you strength, so you're not knocked down so easily and your recovery is swift.

If you are growing and maturing, you should not be the same woman at fifty that you were at age twenty-five.

Always seek wisdom, so you can avoid problems yet solve them when they can't be avoided.

In today's society, a great deal of time is being given to external things but none to internal change.

It does not matter if your nails are stunning and your feet are smooth from the perfect pedicure if you have no peace.

You can be dressed in designer labels from head to toe and yet your home is in turmoil.

Your eyebrows and hair are flawless, and your makeup is perfection yet you have not dealt with your insecurities, and you're still battling low self-esteem.

Your outward appearance is just a mask to cover your truth.

I remember in my job capacity having to visit the home of one of my students. I remember how impressed I was with the yard. The flowers were beautiful; the grass was full and flawless. It almost looked like a plush carpet; it was so well taken care of. I knew this house would be beautiful, neat, clean and, flawless.

When I walked in, the first thing I noticed was the smell of animals. There were two litter boxes in the living room that had not been emptied in a few days. There were dirty dishes on the coffee table with half-eaten food and drinks. There was more disarray and my confusion was is the person that takes care of the yard the same person that lives in the house?

I commented on the beauty of the yard and asked who does their lawn. Mom proudly says, "Oh, their dad. Our neighbors are always saying how beautiful everything looks!"

This is a classic example of fixing the exterior while leaving the interior a hot mess. This becomes a way of life. Your outward self that you present to the world has it together, but your inner self is a mess, and you've given up. You have quit and gotten comfortable in your own mess. You spend your time putting out an image of being together while at the same time hiding your disfunction.

You cannot fix what you will not acknowledge. You cannot win if you drop out of the race.

What do you want for yourself? Are you pursuing it, or have you already quit? Is your energy being used to create the appearance of success rather than actual success?

When company comes over, you can shove all the junk in the closet, but eventually you have to open the door and the mess will all fall out again.

You have a decision to make. Do you want to spend the rest of your life living in confusion, clutter, filth, and disfunction? If the answer is no, then you cannot quit.

Don't quit trying to do better. Don't quit learning from your mistakes. Don't quit having standards for yourself and your life. Don't quit making it clear to people what is and is not acceptable to bring into your life. Don't quit growing in knowledge and wisdom.

Things will get better if you just don't quit.

Reflections

Can you be honest with yourself about where you need to improve?

Did you read this book and see everybody's flaw except yours?

Are you open to a new way of handling the choices of your past and the way you will move forward to a brighter future?

What is the first step you will take to be a better version of yourself?

DAY 30

The Men Speak
31 Quotes from Men to Women

This last day is a series of quotes I got from men whose ages range from nineteen years of age to seventy-three.

The book you've just read was written by a woman and directed toward women. I realize that sometimes women, for whatever reason, will give more credibility when a man speaks rather than when a woman speaks. Here are their responses. I asked each of them the same question, and this is what they had to say.

The question was, "*If you could tell women one thing you would like them to know or understand from a man's point of view, what would it be?*"

Age 19

"If you gone give me some (sex) I'm gone take it but that don't mean you my girl you were just something to do. Next."

Age 70

"Put some clothes on and clean up your nasty mouth. I'm so sick of foul mouth women."

Age 33

"When you tell a man no you shouldn't have to explain or justify it. If he won't take no for an answer you might have a problem with that man."

Age 53

"If you come at me like the only thing you got to offer me is sex, why do you get mad when you get screwed and screwed over. You made the rules and you mad at me for playing the game better than you."

Age 66

"Stop trying to be a woman before it's your time. You need to be a girl before you can be a woman. Slow down you'll get there."

Age 32

"Have some self-confidence. Don't worry about how many women I'm talking to. Be the woman I want to keep talking to."

Age 40

"You don't have to show everything. Leave something to the imagination. Oh yeah, and I don't mind the false eyelashes but I shouldn't be able to see they fake from outer space. Lighten up at least make them look like they yours."

Age 34

"Learn to be an individual before becoming a partner."

Age 52

"Learn your man and you'll earn your man and he'll work to earn you."

Age 65

"Be careful who you allow in your life and around your children."

Age 53

"Do you know how trifling you look at 6:00 in the evening at the grocery store in your pajamas from the night before and house shoes? Have some class."

Age 64

"Stop settling for less than God has for you."

Age 37

"Stop devaluing yourself. Why do you come so cheap? Know your worth."

Age 33

"Be the person you are trying to meet."

Age 52

"Express your needs rather than your wants. A man that cares about you will try to make sure you have all your needs met. He recognizes his role as a provider. He will try to supply all your needs and some of your wants."

Age 70

"Be the age you are. There is nothing more pathetic than a 60-year-old woman trying to act 25, dress 25 and compete with 25-year-olds."

Age 71

"If you want to be treated like a lady, act like one."

Age 36

"Don't put all men in one box. We are individuals."

Age 36

"Unload your baggage from one relationship before you start another one."

Age 62

"A man can be strong but that doesn't mean that things in life don't hurt and affect us too. Sometimes we need your support just like you need ours."

Age 54

"The Bible says when a man findeth a wife he findeth a good thing and obtained favor from the Lord. Sisters be that woman worth finding."

Age 70

"If I don't like who is sitting across the table from me eventually, I won't want you across from me in my bed either."

Age 20

"Don't get mad at me for not respecting you when you don't even respect yourself. If you come correct, I will too."

Age 30

If you are a nothing woman (no goals) that ain't about nothing (doing nothing with your life) then a man won't have a problem giving you nothing and doing nothing because he sees you as a nothing." This one I had to have explained to me which is why I added the part in parentheses. He was saying if you are not working toward a better life for yourself, why should he try to elevate your life?

Age 45

"Trust takes years to build, seconds to destroy and forever to repair."

Age 39

"Not every man that is nice to you is flirting with you, some mothers raised their sons to be respectful gentlemen."

Age 46

"When you tell me about what you do to some other dude when you got mad at him, I'm listening hard. You're telling me how crazy you are and how far you will go to get even."

Age 21

"If you get ghosted, catch a clue. I don't want you."

Age 37

"If I've done something you don't like, instead of having an attitude, talk to me and let resolve the problem."

ABOUT THE AUTHOR

Everybody just calls her Sheila, except at work. She's very casual and loves a relaxed environment and good conversation. She thought about how she would describe herself and realized at each phase of her life that description would change. When she was in high school, she would have been considered a "goody-two-shoes." She has never been someone who follows what others think she should do to receive their approval. This can cause her to be an outcast sometimes. This is when she discovered that liking herself was more important to her than you liking her.

Sheila been a single mother, a stepmother, a married woman, and a divorced woman.

She's been so broke she was living paycheck to prayer and in a place where money was not an issue and she could relax financially.

She, like most women, has had good and bad relationships. She's had her heart broken and friends disappoint her, but through it all, she kept moving forward. When she was weak, God has been her strength. She loves the Lord and believes He loves her unconditionally. Yet she still has expectations on how she represents Christ in her life.

She believes everyone makes mistakes, and her goal is to learn the lesson from each of them. If she had a motto, it would be, "Let every mistake teach you a lesson, and let every lesson teach you not to repeat the same mistakes."

Remember this—a mistake made over and over again stops being a mistake and becomes a choice. She doesn't believe in asking to be rescued for choices she made for herself, so she lives her life trying to choose wisely.

Her hope is this book imparts some of the wisdom she's gained through life experiences.

CPSIA information can be obtained
at www.ICGtesting.com
Printed in the USA
LVHW101519040422
715262LV00005B/228

9 781638 857815